HUMUS

deep soil for life

Veronika Bond

HUMUS

the black gold of the earth

a book about

an endangered species

and things we can do to save it

Title: HUMUS

Subtitle: the black gold of the earth

Author: Veronika Bond

Editor: Joshua Bond

Cover design: Savannah Theis

Publisher: Tredition

Website: www.thehumusproject.org

© 2018 Veronika Bond

The material presented in this book is intended for educational purposes only. No expressed or implied guarantee of the effects of the use of the recommendations can be given nor liability taken by the author.

978-3-7469-2067-2 (Paperback)
978-3-7469-2068-9 (Hardcover)
978-3-7469-2069-6 (e-Book)

to the soil mother

and to my mother

Humus is the real black gold.

~ Friedensreich Hundertwasser ~

Contents

by inspiration – The right conditions for humification

The rapid loss of humus – Natural and manmade erosion – The feeding habits of plants – Destruction and exploitation – Domino effects – The real value of humus

The creativity of humus – Understanding compost as a medium – Experimenting with compost – Art is more than technique – Growing your own mixed media – The greatest of all crafts

Reverence for the earthworm – Earthworms as soil builders – Breeding earthworms – The gold standard of humus – An entourage of loyal supporters

Tools for earthworms – Nutrients for plants – Medicine for the forest – Food for the soil – Sustenance for life – Detox for the garden

Prologue

If the soil is ill, all living beings suffer. The remedy must start there.

~ Maye Bruce ~

In October 2017 a firestorm swept across Central Portugal. Approximately two thirds of the area was burned, most of it in one single night. Within a few hours, miles and miles of countryside, forests, houses, people, animals, livestock, small holdings, gardens, livelihoods were consumed by flames.

How could that happen? Apparently '500 *fires started on Sunday night independently of each other and got out of control because of Hurricane Ophelia coming over the Atlantic'*. But 500 fires don't start spontaneously like that, not even in soaring temperatures at the height of summer.

Was it human negligence? Was it arson? Are the eucalyptus plantations in this area the root cause of the problem? Many questions remain open.

Then the second wave of questions came: *Will this happen again? Can we do anything to stop this and protect ourselves? What, if anything, can we do to prevent this from happening in the future?*

The morning after the firestorm I built a new compost heap. The air was filled with smoke and ashes. In the woodlands next to our house and across the road small 'volcanoes' were still smouldering, spewing fumes and flames. Arranging organic materials from piles which had miraculously survived the fire was the most comforting activity of the moment.

They say, the soil is more fertile after a fire. But, what if there is no soil left? We see black pines and olive trees stripped bare, collapsed on top of the skeleton of rocks, the naked bones of the earth mother exposed.

Two months after the fateful night I read a headline in The Guardian – **Mass starvation is humanity's fate if we keep flogging the land to death**. In the article, George Monbiot points out that "*the trouble begins where everything begins: with soil. The UN's famous projection that, at current rates of soil loss, the world has 60 years of harvests left, appears to be supported by a new set of figures.*"

In other words, when 'the world has no harvests left' there will be no fertile soil, no crops, no food, no fodder, no animals, no trees, no materials to burn. The earth will be *'burnt out'*.

Fires of increasing ferocity and voracity are flaring up all over the world. Think of Australia, California, Italy, Spain, Tasmania... These are not 'natural wildfires'. They contribute to the loss of fertile soil in many ways. Other causes for soil erosion are the use of chemical fertilisers and pesticides, deep ploughing, deforestation, overgrazing and last but not least our personal food habits.

10 years ago my husband and I bought a Quinta in Portugal, partly because we wanted to have a go at growing our own food. In the night of the firestorm, many lives were changed. For us, it catalysed a fundamental change of perception. An old key question had been: *How can we grow more food during more months of the year?*

From the ashes of disaster a more burning question has arisen: *How can we help our soil mother recover and heal her suffering?*

This book is written in response to that new question. The soil is the mother of all living creatures. The olive trees, sheep, farms, humans who lost their lives in the fire and those who survived that tragic night – we are all her children. What can we do to make sure our soil doesn't get reduced to ashes – or dust – as the case may be? Our very existence depends on finding answers to this question, fast.

The Buddhists say, '*all suffering can be healed through understanding*.' This book is a contribution towards *a better understanding of soil as a living organism*. An improved understanding of another living being is the foundation for any healthy relationship. 'HUMUS, *the black gold of the earth*' is primarily about earth, soil, compost and of course *humus*, the lifeblood of the living soil. Paraphrasing Amy Stewart, '*there is more to humus than what we can see, much more. To know the soil mother for what she is, to find her heartbeat, to expose her soul, you have to go underground where she lives and breathes*.'

'HUMUS' is also about humans as guardians of the soil. Humans are intimately related to humus in more ways than most of us currently realise. Researching materials for this book, following the trails of many pioneers and visionaries who knew about this inseparable link, has been a true eye-opener and an inspiration.

I don't have all the answers to the questions listed above. I did, however, find valuable information from sources which are not easily accessible to many readers. Several 'humus-pioneers' from German speaking countries (published 50-100 years ago) have not been translated into English. Several important ecologists from English speaking countries (also writing in that era) have almost been forgotten. To keep their voices alive is one of the aims of this book.

In 2015 the FAO (the United Nations Food and Agriculture Organisation) declared that, "*the main problem humanity is currently facing is not global warming, extinction of species or any other environmental crisis – the main problem we will have to face is the degradation of our soils. The world population continues to increase while we destroy more and more topsoil. If this is allowed to continue there won't be enough fertile soil left to feed a growing world population.*"

Can you imagine the Earth 60 years from 2015, with no soil left to grow any food at all? I like to imagine sparks of inspiration flying across the humus-sphere, lighting cozy fires in winter all over the Earth and ensuring that our grandchildren and great-grandchildren can still cook a healthy, nutritious soup in 2075 and beyond.

Veronika Bond, Portugal, January 2018

Introduction

Put your faith in the two inches of humus, that will build under the trees, every thousand years.

~ Wendell Berry ~

It's not petroleum, nor a rare mineral or a noble metal. The most precious substance in the earth is humus. Humus gives life to the earth. It keeps the soil healthy. Good humus produces strong healthy plants, and healthy plants provide food for healthy animals and humans.

What exactly is humus?

Why is it so precious?

How is it made?

How is it lost?

What is the secret of healthy humus?

These are some of the questions we explore in this book. Of course, almost every gardening book has a section about humus. Do we need another book on such a basic topic?

Gardeners and farmers usually describe humus from a material perspective. They talk about its composition: well-rotted plants and animal manure, rich in minerals and trace elements, with lots of microorganisms in it etc. Such a description gives the impression that humus is mostly 'dead matter', inhabited by relatively insignificant tiny creatures. This idea is confirmed when contemporary soil scientists call humus *'the very dead'*.

Not everybody sees it that way. Lady Eve Balfour, the founder of the British Soil Association, was convinced that humus is *"far from dead...It is still organic matter, in the transition stage between one form of life and another."* And Sir Albert Howard, founder of the organic movement, taught that *'humus is alive, and it makes the soil alive.'*

Is it very dead, or very alive? – such fundamental disagreements can only be explained by radically different perspectives. Some people look at humus through the lens of a microscope and try to grasp it 'objectively' by identifying its chemical and physical components. Others experience its miraculous life-giving and fertilising powers and understand the crucial part humus plays in the life-cycles of the Earth.

This book explores humus as a living organism, a vital

organ of a living earth. Humus plays an essential role in the health of our soil and all life on our planet. Many people concerned about their health want to eat 'healthy organic food' and drink 'pure healthy water'. Not so many think about the key role of healthy soil.

We are so used to defining humus as a material substance – an 'end product of the decomposition process of plant and animal matter' – that seeing it as a 'living organism' is not easy. On the other hand, if we define humans in terms of their material composition – bones and muscles, organs and nervous tissue, blood and lymphatic fluid etc. all enclosed in a bag of skin, partially covered in hair – we can readily accept that this clearly doesn't capture the essence of humanness. A living organism is far more than the sum of its parts. A description of it in purely chemical elements, physical structure and physiological functions can never do it justice. This is partly because our language often lacks the right words to convey the difference between aliveness and deadness.

In this book, we want to get to know live humus a little better. We look at its functions as a 'soil-organism' and the effects it has on plants, animals and humans. We want to find out why it is important for *our* survival, and how we can protect it and ensure *its* survival. We'll meet a number of 'composting artists' who have dedicated their lives to the regeneration of the soil and know a thing or two about how to stimulate the creation of humus. We shall discover that humus is not 'very dead' – at least not yet...

Most importantly, we want to get to know humus as a living being, or more accurately, as a *species of living creatures*. Humuses (plural of humus) can live for millions of years. They can be very young, mature, or ancient. They occur in all climate zones, and their geological background is quite diverse. What makes us assume that an ancient humus of a Russian grassland, a medieval humus in a German monastery garden and a 'young' 70-year-old humus on a biodynamic farm in Australia are '*the same beast*'? Depending on their maturity, nourishment and living conditions, humuses show distinctive personalities and behaviour. They vary in appearance, stability, resilience and fertility.

Humus should be considered an endangered species. According to the *Global Agriculture Report*, "*More than 24 billion tons of soil are lost each year through erosion – that is more than 3 tons of soil per inhabitant of the planet!*" It is true, the soil currently erodes much faster than it regenerates itself. Moreover, the authors of this report call fertile soil '*our most significant non-renewable geo-resource.*' This means we should be very concerned about the disappearance of the soil altogether. It almost sounds as if a major 'soil crisis' is inevitable.

However, '*non-renewable*' can be a misleading

description. Our ancestors knew how to regenerate and renew the soil. People have done this for thousands of years all over the world. If a major soil crisis is looming, everyone should know what they can do to promote the renewal of our most indispensable, most precious geo-resource! In chapter 4 we'll examine why soil – and humus – are lost, how this happens, and what we can do to protect and cultivate it.

Humans are certainly capable of destroying fertile soil, but *we can also help to renew it*. We can learn about the re-creation of humus, and what our recycling habits have to do with it. Anyone who has a garden and wants to 'do something for the environment' can collect their kitchen waste and start a compost pile. This book includes tips and recipes for building a *healthy compost* because creating healthy humus often starts with a skilful arrangement of the materials you want to decompose.

The actual making of healthy humus is the work of billions of microorganisms and thousands of earthworms. Whether you have a garden or not, you can start your own worm farm. Or you can learn about *fermenting* your kitchen waste, or try other simple composting methods and find out what works for you. Almost anyone can contribute to the regeneration of rich fertile soil.

Last but not least, we want to understand – and hopefully improve – the intimate relationship between *humus* and *humans*, because "*understanding the soil is the key to sustainability*," as Howard-Yana Shapiro and John Harrison write in their book *Gardening for the Future of the Earth*. The love affair between *humus* and *human* begins with the name. Both words come from the same Latin root, meaning *earth*. As living organisms, the two have a lot more in common than one might think. When we realise that humus is not only a vital part of our food cycle and a critical basis for our health, but also our distant relative, inseparably tied up with our destiny, perhaps it helps us rebuild the relationship we once had with our '*mother substance*'.

Chapter 1

The Earth Kingdom

When a gardener takes a handful of earth from one of his beds, he holds a world in his hands.

~ Marie Luise Kreuter ~

A brief history of humus

The word *humus* has been around for more than 2000 years. The Roman poet Virgil (70 – 19 B.C.E.) used it in the sense of '*earth*'. Not much later the Latin-speaking people abandoned the term and replaced it with *terra*, which is still the common name for *earth* in Portuguese.

In the 18th century, the word *humus* reappeared in German, when the physician and agronomist Albrecht Thaer began to use it in the sense of a part of the soil: "*The usual name for this substance is mould,*" he explained. "*Humus is the residue of animal and plant putrefaction.*"

By 1925 the term was in common use in other countries too. The Ukrainian-American micro-biologist Selman Waksman wrote that "*several theories have been proposed at various times to explain the origin of the black-coloured organic substances, ... which are commonly known as 'humus'.*" The Austrian philosopher Rudolf Steiner spoke about humus in his lectures on biodynamic farming, and the English botanist Sir Albert Howard recognised the significance of humus for soil fertility and health while managing an organic farm in India (1924 - 1931).

During the 20th century, organic and biodynamic farmers put new 'humus-theories' into practice. They opposed the so-called 'green revolution' – promoting the use of artificial fertilisers and pesticides – and developed new methods for producing humus from organic materials.

The substance itself, of course, *has been around for millions of years.* Planet Earth is 'girdled by a *humus-belt'* which covers large areas in Eastern Europe and Asia, stretches across North American prairies and reappears briefly in Morocco before fading into the Saharan desert. Moldova and Ukraine belong to a part of the world which can be considered the '*cradle of the humus-belt'*.

To raise awareness of our rich and diverse soils, the *International Year of Planet Earth* was established at the turn of the millennium. *The Black Earth* (published in 2011) is a contribution to this program. The book was written by Igori Krupenikov, a renowned soil scientist from Moldova, and his Ukrainian colleague Boris Boincean. Before humans began to plough the land, most of Moldova was covered in black humus-rich soil, often 1 metre deep. The virgin soil was famous for its fertility and used to produce an abundant and diverse variety of crops. Today Moldova is the poorest country in Europe, and the humus-belt is vanishing.

In recognition of the worldwide soil crisis, the *International Year of Soils* was declared by the UN in 2015. Many initiatives sprang up in response to this call, as if many seeds had been lying dormant in the soil.

In June 2015 a group of 60 seasoned ecologists, scientists and soil-pioneers got together in Costa Rica and founded an international alliance called *Regeneration International.* In December 2015 the IUSS (International Union of Soil Science) saw the need for a longer period and declared the *International Decade of Soils*, to last until 2024.

During the first meeting of *Regeneration International* in Costa Rica, Ronnie Cummins, director of the American *Organic Consumers Association*, expressed the need for a *"massive grass roots army of earth-regenerators: 3 billion small farmers, villagers, ranchers, shepherds, forest dwellers, urban gardeners* and indigenous communities – assisted by several billions of conscious consumers and urban activists."

Before we can do anything to help stop, and maybe even reverse the rapid degeneration of our soils, we need to understand what this 'stuff under our feet' actually is. "We know more about the movement of celestial bodies than about the soil underfoot," Leonardo da Vinci famously pointed out several centuries ago. Unfortunately, this still seems to be the case, generally speaking. But now there are many people who have studied the soil, and we can learn from them.

Humus gets mixed up

The term *humus* is often confused with topsoil and compost. Even experts write about 'compost' and 'humus' as if they were the same thing. Deploring this mix-up, Lady Eve Balfour stated, "*the term 'giving the land humus' is too often taken as a synonym for treating it with any form of organic matter, such as ploughing in green crops or grass or applying farmyard manure. But all these substances are merely some of the raw materials from which humus can be made. They cannot become humus until they have been metabolised by soil organisms.*"

To add to the confusion, the word 'composting' is often used synonymously with *humification* – i.e. the transformation process of organic materials into humus. *Composting* has a wide range of other meanings too. It can be used in the sense of *putting organic waste into a compost bin.* Or it can mean *taking decomposed substances from the compost pile and digging them into the garden soil.* Moreover, it is not uncommon for experienced gardeners to talk about *humus* (or *compost*) when they actually mean *fertile topsoil.* Not surprisingly, this can leave the gardening novice floundering.

So what exactly is *humus*, and how is it different from *topsoil* and *compost*?

Lady Louise Howard explained it like this: "*Humus is a Latin word meaning soil, but in science its significance is a little narrowed to indicate that part of the soil spread over the surface of the earth which is the end product of the decaying fragments of organic matter.*"

Humus – in the sense used by Thaer, Waksman, Howard and Krupenikov – is considered *a living substance.* It is *transformed compost*, the product of a *healthy decomposition of organic matter.* The use of the term *humus* in contemporary literature is inconsistent. German humus experts make a distinction between *Nährhumus* (nutritional humus) and *Dauerhumus* (permanent or durable humus). Lady Balfour's writings give the impression that the word *humus* entered the English language in both senses despite the lack of precise terms for these different stages of humus development.

American humus experts use the term *compost* in the sense of the German *nutritional humus*. The word *humus* (on its own) is reserved for the so-called *permanent humus*. In this book, we take the European approach and use the word *compost* for the *accumulation of organic substances in earlier stages of decay*.

Inevitably, due to the continuous cycle of dying and living, the boundaries between *compost* and *humus* are blurry, and the better we get to know this creature, the more we'll understand why. To illustrate the fundamental distinction between *compost* and *humus*, we can draw a comparison with the difference between a caterpillar and a butterfly. Compost is the creature in the state of the caterpillar, humus is the same creature in the butterfly stage. Both *humus* and *compost* are present in the *topsoil*. Topsoil, compost and humus do have a lot in common, but they differ in their functions, colour, texture and behaviour. One could argue that they are 'the same beast' at different stages of its development. Let's take a closer look at the 3 terms.

Topsoil

Soil often gets mixed up with another word: *dirt*. This is interesting because the word dirt originally meant '*excrement*', and fertile soil does have a lot to do with the excrements of many creatures. However, dirt has negative associations with uncleanliness, insignificance and humiliation, which can get in the way of appreciating the true value of the soil.

When you dig a hole to plant a tree in the garden you should see various horizontal layers in the earth. The upper cover of healthy soil consists of rotting organic matter. The second cover can be regarded as the actual humus layer. Both layers are populated by beneficial bacteria, earthworms, soil fungi, micro-organisms and many other small creatures. The third layer is composed of many minerals and serves as a reservoir for water and soil nutrients. The first two layers of earth are the topsoil.

Krupenikov and his colleague describe the topsoil as 'the Earth's living skin' covering the Earth's crust and protecting it. "*Far from being an inert membrane, the soil creates local conditions for an immense variety of physical, chemical and biological processes.*" These layers of living tissue are the existential basis for all living creatures, including plants, earthworms ... and humans.

Compost

Compost is literally a composition of many different materials from the plant, animal and mineral kingdoms. In nature, compost occurs as a mix of fresh and decomposing organic matter: autumn leaves, wilted flowers, dead insects, broken twigs and branches, urine and faeces from animals, small stones, rock dust, empty snail shells, etc. This means, compost is not homogenous. Being an accumulation of mainly vegetable and animal matter in various stages of decay it has a mixed texture.

Christa Weinrich, Benedictine nun and head gardener at the Abbey of Fulda (Germany) – calls the compost heap the 'heart of the garden'. At the same time, compost often relates to 'a collection of organic waste': vegetable scraps from the kitchen, grass clippings from the lawn, hedge cuttings etc. In other words, it refers to a particular type of 'recyclable rubbish'.

For a clearer understanding of compost, we must differentiate between the random accumulation of organic waste and the skilful composition of decaying organic materials. Both can be called 'compost'. A random accumulation of scraps from the kitchen can fester, attract unwanted animals and turn into a stinking, repulsive mass. Surely, this doesn't happen in the 'heart of the monastery garden' at Fulda (!) which has been cultivated organically by Benedictine nuns for 500 years.

A skilful composition of vegetable matter, animal manure and minerals attracts desirable creatures which stimulate a healthy decomposition process. A 'good compost' doesn't smell bad. It becomes a valuable production-plant for humus which regenerates the lifeblood of the topsoil. This compost is a very valuable resource, treasured by all gardeners.

Humus

Humus has the colour of dark chocolate. It is homogenous, it has the texture of a moist and crumbly cake and a characteristic earthy smell. Humus is *transformed compost*, metabolised by earthworms and other microorganisms living in the soil. Waksman described humus as a *'natural body'*. "*It is a composite entity, just as are plant-, animal- and microbial substances; it is even much more complex chemically, since all these materials contribute to its formation.*" Because humus is 'made up' from so many different sources and occurs in very different environments, it can vary a lot.

Sir Howard knew that, "*humus cannot be exactly the same thing everywhere. It is bound to be a creature of circumstance.*" Some soil scientists have tried to nail down humus by defining it as a 'stable substance', the 'end product of a metabolic process' but this turned out to be incorrect. In Sir Howard's understanding "*humus in the natural state is dynamic, not static.*"

Soil scientists and farmers have difficulty in agreeing what humus is because the interpretation depends on a fundamental outlook on life itself. The American soil specialist Paul Sachs suspects the problem might be due to a lack of precision. "*Humus is complex, and even after hundreds of years of research, no one really knows exactly what it is.*", he explains. "*The term humus doesn't really describe anything specific. It's like using the word 'dog' to describe a German Short Haired Pointer or a Russian wolfhound.*"

As previously mentioned, German humus experts distinguish between nutritional humus and permanent humus. Let's call them '*nutri-humus*' and '*perma-humus*'. These terms describe two different stages of humus development. Nutri-humus is a younger version of perma-humus. The upper layer of the topsoil contains more nutri-humus, while the second layer is saturated with the older, more mature and 'stable' perma-humus. Nutri-humus is rich in nutrients which are released quickly for plant growth. In cultivated soil, it only lasts for one growing season and needs to be replenished on a regular basis. Perma-humus can survive for hundreds of years.

Marie Luise Kreuter, Germany's 'organic gardener of the nation', explains it like this: "*The two upper soil layers are not only distinguishable by their different populations and their ways of working. Also, the humus in these two parts is of a different kind. Fertile soil is produced in the upper rotting layer, which always regrows. But it is relatively short-lived... under unfavourable conditions, this humus can be destroyed.*"

By contrast, the so-called perma-humus occurs in the lower actual humus layer...The soil crumbs are smaller here, more intensely connected and more stable... When in rich supply, they produce a nitrogen reservoir in the soil which mineralises the nutrients gradually to pass them on to the plants."

The very alive

Taking into account the vitalising effects humus has on soil, plants, animals and humans, it is hard to understand why anyone would call it 'very dead'. Humus seems very alive. In some schools of soil science, it is even classed as a species. Many eminent scientists, expert farmers and master gardeners talk about the black gold in the topsoil as if it was a kind of living creature. Vasily Dokuchaev, a Russian geologist and deemed the founder of soil science, perceived humus-rich soils as *'individual natural bodies'*. He even suggested to classify them as *"the '4th kingdom of nature', in a league with minerals, plants and animals."*

It is a valid suggestion. Humus has some characteristic features of a living creature:

- Humus goes through distinct stages of development, from the fetal composting phase, through the infantile and adolescent phases of nutri-humus, which still has some resemblance with compost, to the adult phase of perma-humus.

- As humus grows and matures, it becomes more resilient, it is able to store, manage and share its resources better, and it becomes a more 'stable creature'.

- Humus is very fertile and has the ability to reproduce. It regenerates itself unless its fertility is destroyed through adverse conditions.

As a species, humus has many breeds. Different breeds of humus have their own personalities, dispositions and dietary requirements. Like other life forms, not all breeds of humus are at home in the same climate, and they respond to specific environmental factors.

Moreover, *humus is full of life*. It provides a home for millions of species of microorganisms. This is why we can read in many gardening books that '*a handful of fertile soil contains more living creatures than the whole human population of planet Earth*'.

Chapter 2

The Soil Mother

To forget how to dig the earth and to tend the soil is to forget ourselves.

~ Mahatma Gandhi ~

Mother soil

In German *humus* is also called *Mutterboden* which literally means 'mother soil'. Perhaps the word comes from the instinctive knowledge of the people that *humus-rich soil is the mother substance of all life on earth.* The soil mother looks after her children from the plant-, mineral- and animal kingdoms with natural maternal instincts. What she offers freely, however, is sometimes hard to recognise and appreciate. When gifts are forgotten or taken for granted they lose their value. Through neglect and ignorance, the generous gifts of the soil mother are now dwindling fast. So let's remind ourselves of some of the precious offerings of humus to all living beings on Earth: *fertility, protection, balance, stability, energy, food* and *health.*

Humus gives fertility

The 'soil mother' makes the earth fertile and productive. Fertilisers – both the synthetic and organic varieties – are used to promote the growth of plants and produce a good harvest. These substances have to be applied in every growing season, often more than once. They give a short-term superficial fertility boost. Humus, by contrast, ensures the soil's long-term fertility. Some types of humus give fertility to the soil for 100s or even 1000s of years.

Humus gives protection

The soil mother protects the earth from harm, disease and death. Humans have developed synthetic pesticides and organic remedies to protect plants against attacks from pests and cure their diseases. We have also invented irrigation and drainage systems to protect our land against flooding and drought.

Humus builds the immune system of the soil, which offers protection in a wide range of potentially hazardous situations, not only for the benefit of the vegetable kingdom. Humus inoculates the earth with healthy organisms. This strengthens the plants and gives them immunity, so they can grow their own resilience against pests, parasites, viruses and other harmful influences. This immunity is transferred to animals and humans who eat the plants. (See *Humus gives health*). Moreover, humus protects the soil against drought and flooding. (More about that in the next paragraph).

Humus gives balance

The soil mother regulates the general living conditions in the earth. We know that plants like growing in soils which are neither too acidic nor too alkaline. Plants, and all other life forms can only survive within a neutral range, which can be measured as the so-called *pH-value* (pH is short for 'pondus hydrogenii', and this refers to the 'weight of hydrogen ions' in the soil). We can do soil tests and add certain substances to 'get the pH level right'. Humus, as a living organism, adapts to the needs of the plants and regulates the pH level. Somehow the soil mother knows how to find the right balance.

Humus regulates air flow and water contents in the topsoil. In his book on earthworms, Charles Darwin wrote that humus-rich soil has an increased capacity to absorb and hold water, which is due to the constant work of the worms in the earth. (This insight was already available in the late 19th century, but his book on earthworms didn't catch on at the time).

Humus also helps to improve the drainage of surplus water from the topsoil, again, thanks to the numerous small tunnels made by the earthworms. Additionally, humus helps to regulate the temperature in the soil and protects the underground life from extreme heat or cold.

Humus gives stability

The soil mother provides a solid foundation for all life forms on Earth. Without humus the soil turns to dust and becomes a desert. Plants, animals and humans literally desert the inhospitable place. Humus arranges the topsoil in ways beneficial for plant growth. It acts like a glue holding the dust together, without turning it into a solid impenetrable mass. The soil scientists Igori Krupenikov and Boris Boincean call earthworms "*the chief architects and builders*" of the humus-rich soil. Millions of earthworms constantly burrow their tiny tunnels through the earth kingdom. They produce humus – the building material of the soil – and create safe and complex architectural structures to house the fragile subterranean life processes.

Humus gives energy

The soil mother stores solar energy. Plants have direct access to the sun's energy, they are able to use it for their own vital processes, and this energy is passed on to the humus. Some of it becomes available to animals and humans in the form of edible vegetable matter grown in humus-rich soils. But a lot of it remains unused and gets wasted. The American soil expert Paul Sachs writes, *"humus is essentially a massive storage battery containing energy that was originally derived from the sun. Researchers in England discovered that an acre (4500 square meters) of soil with 4 percent organic matter contains as much energy as 20-25 tons of anthracite coal."*

Krupenikov and Boincean confirm that *"soil organic matter* (a current scientific term for humus) *makes up about three-quarters of global stocks of organic carbon.... Soil organic matter is the biggest carbon store that we know how to manage."* So far this huge energy store in the soil has largely been overlooked, underestimated, or destroyed. The two soil scientists propose a *'new ecological paradigm'* built on optimal recycling of energy and nutrients to ensure the regeneration of humus as a renewable resource.

Humus gives food

The soil mother feeds all living creatures on planet Earth. Humus provides plants with all essential nutrients: carbon, nitrogen, phosphorus, potassium, calcium, magnesium, iron, ... the list goes on. Again, humans have figured out how to synthesise these elements and feed them directly to the plants, but the effects have been fatal. Chemical fertilisers are directly linked to loss of humus, loss of soil fertility, soil erosion, and rising suicide rates among farmers. Manmade cocktails of so-called 'plant nutrients' obviously cannot replicate what the Earth does naturally and perfectly. Humus provides all the food we need to feed plants, animals, humans and the soil itself. The soil mother makes sure that the food cycle remains unbroken.

Humus gives health

The soil mother looks after the wellbeing of all life forms and of the Earth itself. Hippocrates already said it 2500 years ago: the health of the people depends on the health of the soil. When Sir Albert Howard was managing his organic farm in India he could see that humus-rich soils produce healthy plants. He didn't need to protect his crops against pests and diseases because they were immunised by healthy humus. He also observed that this healthy crop kept the cattle healthy. They didn't need to be treated with antibiotics and other toxic drugs. He suspected that *the health and well-being of mankind must depend on the efficiency of the mycorrhizal association between soil fungi and plant roots.*

Lady Eve Balfour became a great fan of Sir Albert's new methods of making organic humus. She had suffered from recurring colds and painful rheumatism for as long as she could remember. In the winter of 1938-39, she ate only homemade bread baked from whole wheat grown in humus-rich soil. *"That winter,"* she shares with delight, *"I had no colds at all, and almost for the first time in my life I was free from rheumatic pains even in prolonged spells of wet weather."*

Humus gives life

In 1892 a young Austrian-Hungarian microbiologist started studying the plankton of the Plattensee. His name was Raoul Heinrich Francé. He began to publish papers on topics such as *the life of algae*, *the organisation of flagellates* and *marine worms*.

Francé's work attracted the attention of the Royal Hungarian Society of Natural Sciences, and he was commissioned to research the soil of moorlands. This project gave him an opportunity to study the soil life, and these studies became the foundation for his life's work.

In 1913 the first edition of Raoul Francé's seminal book about the life of the soil was published in Munich. The work was ground breaking 100 years ago – both literally and figuratively. It offers unique insights into the inner life of humus which remains relevant to this day. Even though most of his books are currently either out of print, or only available in German, Francé plays a major part in our understanding of the soil.

Chapter 3

The Creation of Humus

The forest creates even the soil on which it lives, according to its requirements; many metres deep it accumulates the jungle-humus and protects the flanks of the mountains against the forces of destruction.

~ Raoul H. Francé ~

The Edaphon

Raoul Francé (1874-1943) discovered that the microorganisms in the soil fulfil a function similar to the plankton in oceans, lakes and rivers. His logical conclusion was to give the soil population a collective name, and he called them *edaphon*. The edaphon includes bacteria, algae, soil fungi, amoeba, springtails, insects, nematodes, ants, earthworms, wood-lice, centipedes, spiders and many more. All these creatures live in close relationships with each other, and they maintain the equilibrium, health and structure of the humus-body.

The edaphon embodies the 'life and vitality' of humus. From the perspective of reductionist materialism (the theory that life can be reduced to physical matter), these microorganisms 'populate the soil'. When we regard humus as a living being, however, it becomes obvious that *they are part of the living tissue of the humus-body.*

One of the main functions of the edaphon is the continuous regeneration of the living tissue of humus. Only because we can identify the tiny soil fauna as 'independent specimens of the animal kingdom', this doesn't mean they can exist independently. They can't survive without one another. Without them, humus would disappear. There would be no fertile soil. With the edaphon new life is created from so-called 'dead matter'.

Humus: a slow act of creation

In its natural environment, humus is created continuously through the transformation of organic matter. Some of the humus reserves of the Earth have built up over millennia. In the wild – i.e. in soil not cultivated by humans – this natural regeneration process is very slow. It can take 1000 years for compostable materials to turn into 2.5 centimetres (1 inch) of humus.

Igori Krupenikov and Boris Boincean admit that soil science cannot explain the creation of humus as such. *"The soul of the soil is the continuous process of transformation of organic matter. We are far from understanding all of its complex interactions but, at our present level of comprehension, the important thing is to create the right conditions for this process."*

Marie Luise Kreuter called the creation of humus a *'resurrection.'* When dead plants and animals decay they fall apart, into an apparent chaos and become a source of renewal, fertility and vitality. In other words, the creation of humus represents the quintessential cycle of life and death. The decomposition is catalysed by living creatures, most of them microscopically tiny – that's why they are called *microorganisms*. Organic gardeners and biodynamic farmers are continuously experimenting with creating the right conditions for the transformative process of compost into humus. Depending on various factors, high-quality humus can be produced from a combination of organic materials within a few short months, or even weeks, although speed is not necessarily of the essence.

Organic humus by observation

Sir Albert Howard developed an organic composting method which is still used by many organic farmers and gardeners today. With the so-called *'Indore composting method*' (named after the location of the farm near a place in India called Indore) a compost pile was transformed into organic humus within about 3 months. In his book *An Agricultural Testament* Sir Albert explains the Indore process in detail: *The raw materials are agricultural waste, prunings, wood shavings, bracken, animal bedding etc. plus manure from cattle, 'animal residues' including bones and earth from the stables (which is soaked with animal urine). The urine acts as a compost activator. It stimulates the transformation process and speeds it up considerably.*

For a skilful composition of organic matter, you need a considerable amount of dry and fresh plant materials – normally about 1 cubic meter for building a successful compost. If a farm or garden does not have enough plant materials, Sir Albert suggests a more effective use of the land by "*growing plants for composting on every possible square foot of soil.*"

Many additional factors must be taken into account as well, including the climate and the size of the compost heap (at Indore a compost heap measures 30 x 14 x 3 feet = about 9 x 4 x 1 m). To ensure a healthy decomposition process the compost has to be constructed in layers, the right proportion of carbon-rich and nitrogen-rich materials is important, the heap must never get too wet or too dry, and good aeration is essential. After 2-3 weeks the compost heap is turned over with a pitch fork and watered if necessary. One month and 2 months after setting up the compost pile it is turned a second and a third time respectively. Under favourable conditions this material is transformed into the highly sought after 'black gold' within approximately 12 weeks. (The description of this process relates of course to humus created in India, where climate conditions also stimulate a fast transformation. A more detailed description of the Indore Organic Compost is included in the appendix).

Biodynamic humus by inspiration

In his *Agriculture Course*, Rudolf Steiner introduced some preparations the audience had never heard of. For example, he suggested to stuff cow horns with cow manure, put yarrow blossoms into a stag's bladder, fill an animal's skull with chopped oak bark, etc. Rudolf Steiner was a philosopher with a clairvoyant gift. He wasn't a farmer. However, he had received certain recipes by inspiration and taught farmers how to make six special *biodynamic preparations*. He also gave instructions *when* to bury the preparations '*in the fertile layer of the earth*' and how long to leave them there. Taking planetary influences into consideration, the preparations should be dug up in spring (or in another designated season) and were ready to be used '*in homoeopathic doses*' to activate a large compost pile, or to be spread over a whole field.

Biodynamic Farmers have created and used these preparations since the 1920s, sometimes with astonishing results. While the method sounds somewhat obscure, the fertile soils and healthy crops produced through skilful treatment with the biodynamic preparations – and applied by a true master – speak for themselves.

After the second world war, Alex Podolinsky emigrated to Australia and became a pioneer of biodynamic farming. With the help of the 'BD preparations,' he brought thousands of acres of dead soil back to life. He became an inspiration for many farmers in Australia – and worldwide. After attending a course in Italy one course member wrote: "I *count myself very lucky to have been able to hear Alex Podolinsky's lecture and then to see his teaching so effectively applied at Agrilatina. That soil transformation was a miracle! I have never seen anything like it!*"

The right conditions for humification

But how exactly does a compost heap become humus?

What are the right conditions for the metamorphosis of the 'rotting beast' into a desirable creature?

Humification – that's the official name for the transformation of dead organic matter into live humus – happens in the dark. Oak leaves fall to the ground and decay in the shade of the oak tree. Exposed to rain and fresh air they soon turn black, disintegrate gradually and become part of the soil. Like the oak leaves on the ground, the humification process in the compost heap needs shade, moisture and oxygen. Given these conditions, beneficial bacteria arrive spontaneously and start the work of decomposing.

A mixture of rotting vegetable matter and animal manure soon attracts earthworms from the deeper layers of the soil; somehow they can 'smell' the presence of their favourite food. They dig their way up, grab a fallen leaf and pull it down into their burrows. All decaying substances from the plant and animal kingdoms wander through the digestive channels of these slender stripy creatures. We know that earthworms play a major part in converting compost into humus and that they like working at night. They don't like extreme temperatures and need a continuous supply of food, water and fresh air.

Humification is largely a digestive process. Fresh humus is the stockpile of excretions from thousands of earthworms that have found their way into the compost heap. The worm castings attract millions of microbes, and these continue the humification process. This means the *right conditions for the creation of humus are those which support the crucial activity of beneficial bacteria, earthworms and microbes.*

Humification is a quiet affair with a slow rhythm. Gardeners can tune into this process with their own attitude. Marie Luise Kreuter recommended cultivating the 'old-fashioned virtue of patience'. "*Sometimes it is more important to observe and contemplate, rather than act immediately.*" she writes. "*Pressing a button on a spraying device would be much easier... that would establish peace and order externally, but it would be the peace of a graveyard. The order of sensitive ecological connections is disturbed through such violent measures.*"

Chapter 4

The Extinction of Humus

There are laws against humans killing each other, societies to prevent cruelty to animals, ecology targets plants. Mother Earth is treated like dirt.

~ Alex Podolinsky ~

The rapid loss of humus

Over the past century, about 30-40% of humus has been lost in Moldava, once one of the humus-richest countries in the world. If this trend continues, soil scientists fear that by 2025 there will be no humus left in the Moldovan soil. A rapid loss of humus can be observed worldwide. Loss of humus goes hand in hand with the loss of soil fertility. The British Soil Association warns: "*Already, one quarter of the world's arable soils are severely degraded, and we lose another 30 football pitches worth of soil every minute.*"

Natural and manmade erosion

Soil erosion is, to a certain degree, a natural process. Topsoil gets eroded by wind and rain when there are no plants 'holding it together' with their roots. Storms can blow the soil off sloping grounds, and heavy rains wash it into the sea. In the past 100 years, erosion has been accelerated through human activities, especially deforestation, monoculture and conventional farming methods. Deforestation removes indigenous forests from the land, and the soil is left without the rich organic materials which are the natural sources to replenish the humus.

Monocultures make both plants and soil more vulnerable to disease and erosion. They usually go hand in hand with conventional farming methods, using chemical fertilisers and pesticides which upset the sensitive ecosystem. As a living organism, the soil no longer has access to the diverse range of vegetable matter needed to regenerate itself. Moreover, synthetic fertilisers act like drugs given to the soil. They make the land 'addicted' to the chemical substances, and the soil loses its capacity to produce the vital minerals from within itself. The pesticides are toxic not only to unwanted insects but also the beneficial living creatures in the ground. They kill the essential life forms on which the regeneration of humus depends.

The feeding habits of plants

Plants have two types of roots, some longer, darker more vertical ones, and some smaller, more horizontal, white rootlets. The longer and darker vertical roots allow the plant to absorb water. The small white rootlets are dedicated to the intake of food. The two types of roots play a central role for our understanding of the relationship between plants and humus.

Plant nutrients, i.e. minerals and trace elements, should be absorbed through the white rootlets. All nutrients are contained in healthy humus, and – this is really important – humus is not soluble in water. Alex Podolinsky, the biodynamic farmer from Australia, explains that, *"The first and foremost thing with humus is that it is a colloid. This ball of humus in my hand contains water-soluble salts (minerals). When I place this substance in a glass of water... it would remain like this for months, and the soluble salts present in the humus would not mix with the water, because it is a colloid, which holds the totality of the substance as if enclosed in a skin."*

The colloidal state of humus allows plants to draw specific nutrients from the soil on demand. Adding fertilisers to the soil – of chemical or organic varieties – ignores and overrides this natural function of humus.

Moreover, when fertilisers are added to the soil

independently of humus, then the plant is forced to absorb the mineral-rich water through the 'drinking roots'. It is force-fed a lot more salt, such as nitrates, than it would take in through the 'feeder rootlets'. This happens not only with chemical fertilisers but also when immature compost is added to the soil which has not yet transformed into colloidal humus. As a result, the water household of the plant is disrupted, and the root system gets confused.

"The plant's metabolism is stimulated by the warmth of the sun. The white rootlets are stimulated by solar warmth." Alex Podolinsky explains further. *"The white feeder rootlets enter the humus and absorb water-soluble salts in exact amounts as dictated or inspired by solar warmth."*

With a good supply of humus, plants pick the nutrients they need from the soil and absorb them through their feeder rootlets. This means, humus-rich soil is for the plant like being offered a complete menu of nutrient-rich food with an invitation to eat whatever it wants and needs. When plants are supplied with 'fertilisers' it is like being drip fed selective nutrients into the veins. This is neither a natural nor healthy nourishment. It might be ok in an emergency, but as a long-term measure it has proven to be harmful. It interferes not only with the natural feeding habits of plants but also with the vital functions of humus.

When the plants' root systems get confused, the roots

don't develop properly. And when humus is prevented from fulfilling its function, it begins to degenerate. The soil loses its structure and dries out, or it gets compacted. Then farmers come with heavy farm equipment to break up the hard ground and 'beat the soil into submission', which makes the situation worse.

Destruction and exploitation

It takes hundreds of years – maybe a whole millennium – for the Earth to generate a thin layer of humus-rich topsoil. If 24 billion tons of topsoil are lost each year through erosion, as suggested by the Global Agriculture Report, topsoil is lost much faster than it can regenerate naturally. Human activity is accelerating natural erosion. Bill Mollison, one of the founders of the permaculture movement wrote in 1988, *"Even the most ideal tillage just keeps pace with the most ideal conditions of soil formation, and in **the worst cases we can remove 2000 years of soil in a single erosion season**."*

The Austrian 'rebel farmer' Sepp Holzer adds that, *"The common practice of deep ploughing in the autumn causes the soil to freeze and they both (ploughing and freezing) in turn destroy not only the soil life, but also the natural layering and the build-up of humus."* Even farming with organic methods depletes the humus contents in the soil, because vegetables and cereals absorb nutrients from the humus layer of the soil, and these need to be replenished. In the wild, plants die back and enrich the mother soil with their substance. Cultivated plants, however, are harvested, and the soil often doesn't even get the benefit of those parts of the plants not used for human consumption.

The most fundamental and far reaching reason for the loss of humus-rich topsoil is not so much a matter of specific activities, farming methods, or substances we put in the soil. It is human ignorance and negligence. Soil expert Paul Sachs points out that *"humus is a renewable resource. Its presence in the soil can be maintained indefinitely. Unfortunately, many agricultural and horticultural practices are essentially mining humus. Like other mined products, such as coal, minerals and oil, the natural resource can eventually be exhausted."*

Domino effects

Since humus plays such an important role for our survival on the planet, losing this precious substance has serious implications. The first obvious effect is a loss of topsoil, both in quantity and quality. Then we can notice a marked loss of plant diversity, health and resilience. As the plants lose their vitality, the crops they produce have fewer nutrients. The produce from animals feeding on such plants inevitably loses its quality. This means, with the loss of humus the main natural source of healthy food is vanishing.

The loss of humus also has serious repercussions for our climate. Peter Tompkins and Christopher Bird highlight that, "*Tending the planet's soil may now be our prime priority for an even more urgent reason: to save the world from imminent glaciation. All our healthy topsoil, all the microorganisms in it, and all the plants that thrive thereon, from lichens to the great rainforests, have received their nourishment from millions of tons of mountain rock dust, ground up and washed away by melting glaciers from the last great ice age, some twelve thousand years ago, to be globally spread by whirling windstorms. That life-giving dust is now used up, and our precious topsoil wantonly eroded. Unless something is done to replenish the soil with rock dust, and quickly, warns one group of experts, another great age of ice will do it for us.*"

Although this quote – written in the 1970s – contradicts current theories about global warming, the point about the loss of minerals in the soil, and its effects on the Earth's climate is noteworthy.

The real value of humus

As a result of our general ignorance, the soil is being treated as dirt. However, we can also promote and accelerate the creation of humus and stimulate the regeneration of healthy topsoil. There is already a range of proven methods available. All pioneers in organic gardening, biodynamic farming and permaculture make a commitment to work *with* nature rather than against her. Many of them generously share their knowledge and inspire others to follow their example. The key to regenerating the soil lies in understanding the soil mother as a living organism and treating her accordingly. Instead of viewing compost as 'dead waste' and humus as a 'very dead matter', we can build a personal relationship with the cycle of life and death, be it in one's own garden, allotment, small holding, or even in a flower pot on the window sill.

Paul Sachs reminds us that, *"humus in the soil has more real value than money, real estate, stocks or bonds. Its value doesn't fluctuate; it doesn't become scarce in a recession; it's worth can't be depleted by inflation and it can't be stolen. It is the direct or indirect source of sustenance for all life on earth. It can sometimes be lost by environmental changes, but more often its demise is from either the apathy or the inadvertent errors of the steward who tends it."*

Chapter 5

Composting as an Art Form

Making compost is an extremely creative and personal endeavour.

~ Barbara Pleasant & Deborah Martin ~

The creativity of humus

Compost is better known as a collection of waste materials than as a resource for a creative pursuit. The results of composting, however – the precious living substance we call humus – has long been associated with the act of creation. The physician and practising farmer Albrecht Thaer (1752-1828) had no doubt that humus played not only a central role in the nutrition of plants but also had perceptible creative powers: "As *humus is a life creation it also creates life*," he wrote.

Humus is not only a living substance and a source for life, it is also the result of a creative process. Getting involved in composting means participating in the creative cycle par excellence. *"Whoever wants to learn the creative art of composting should keep reminding themselves that the cycle of substances is not a mechanical process but a miracle of life,"* says Marie Luise Kreuter

Art projects are well known for developing a life of their own. This is especially true for the art of composting. A compost pile literally comes alive by attracting an abundance of living creatures. And like any creative project, it can also go wrong. A compost heap can fail. It can turn into a smelly mess instead of a delicious aromatic crumbly substance. As 'composting artists' we need to be aware of those hazards and understand our medium as well as the creative processes of life and the creatures which readily support our project.

"In a compost heap, there are similar transformation processes as in the humus layer of the soil." Marie Luise Kreuter explains. *"Organic substances are made smaller, their structures are broken up... In the soil as in the compost new earth comes into being... The production of new earth is not only a creative but also a very cultivated activity."*

Understanding compost as a medium

Compostable kitchen waste goes into the bin under the sink. The decaying substances start to rot, go smelly and attract fruit flies. How does this stinking garbage turn into the 'black gold' for the veg patch?

Understanding the creative process of making humus doesn't come by reading a book alone. Getting a grasp on the subject intellectually is a good start, but full understanding needs experience and practice; and experience comes with experimenting, trial and error, playing with different approaches and discovering what works for you.

Barbara Pleasant and Deborah Martin – authors of *The Complete Compost Gardening Guide* – write: *"Making compost is an extremely creative and personal endeavor.... Your compost pile will be as unique as your fingerprints, even if you use the same basic ingredients as your neighbour. Once you're comfortable with the fundamentals of composting, it's fun to explore the boundaries of the process."*

From professional organic gardeners, we can learn that a compost heap should measure about 1 m^3. Organic and biodynamic farmers often build much larger heaps. But, *what if you don't have a big garden or enough materials to fill a whole cubic metre?*

In their book on compost gardening, Barbara Pleasant and Deb Martin introduce a wide range of approaches for 'creative home composting'. The creative process of composting relies on a communal effort of humans and millions of tiny creatures in the soil, and many public spaces are in need of good humus too. Becoming a volunteer in a community garden might be a good way to start learning about and understanding your creative medium.

Experimenting with compost

When Rudolf Steiner gave his lectures on biodynamic agriculture he encouraged his students not to follow his suggestions blindly, but to experiment. Maye Bruce, a keen gardener and founding member of the British Soil Association, joined the anthroposophical society in England in the 1920s; and there she came across the biodynamic preparations. Eight decades before the authors of the *Complete Compost Gardening Guide*, she wanted to make composting more accessible for 'creative home composting'.

"It all started with the garden, a derelict garden, but with beautiful bones..." she remembers. *"The soil was shallow and stony, thin, friable, and very, very hungry."* Maye Bruce became aware of an urgent worldwide need for compost. *"I saw that it was the millions of smallholders, allotment-holders and gardeners who needed it most, for they were quite unable to get farmyard manure. The Steiner Method seemed to me to*

be too complicated to have a universal appeal."

She followed Rudolf Steiner's advice and began to experiment with the plants recommended for the biodynamic preparations: *yarrow, chamomile, dandelion, stinging nettle, valerian* and *oak bark.* One morning she woke up *"with the key to the problem in my mind and the words ringing in my head: 'The Divinity within the flower is sufficient of Itself'."*

The rest is history, as they say. Maye Bruce developed a recipe for a plant powder which accelerates the composting process considerably when added to the compost heap. The nuns at the Abbey of Fulda in Germany worked with Maye Bruce until her death in 1964, and they still produce the plant powder today. In 2009 the recipe was rediscovered in England, where it is now made and sold under the name 'Quick Return Compost Activator'.

Art is more than technique

Making compost heaps is not the only way of creating good humus. In fact, some composting artists are not in favour of it at all. Alex Podolinsky — who is used to working on a large canvas, i.e. farms of up to 4000 hectares — teaches his students to *'read the soil'* and learn to understand what it needs. A living soil doesn't have to be black, but it should be *'luminous like the soil in a painting by Van Gogh,'* he says.

The 'miraculous soil transformation' at the biodynamic farm Agrilatina near Rome didn't happen by gathering tons of organic matter and piling on the humus. The master of biodynamic farming recommended sprinkling biodynamic preparations over the entire farm plus other methods (see chapter 8 *surface compost*), and within less than one year the humus layer in the topsoil began to change.

Creating live humus affects not only the soil but also the water table. It can make water return to a stream that has run dry each summer. After a conventional farm was taken over by a biodynamic 'humus making artist', an 85-year-old neighbour remarked, *"I don't know what you are doing down there, but this is the first time I've seen this stream running all through the summer and autumn in 80 years."*

Growing your own mixed media

As an art form, composting works best in a 'mixed media' composition. There are scores of ways of making humus. The ingredients for a healthy compost heap can vary greatly, depending on location, season, climate zone, available resources and the nature of the land. Ideally, composting artists use materials they find on the land they want to cultivate, since creating new humus and growing plants go hand in hand.

Novice gardeners tend to focus on growing plants to

provide food for their own table. You hear about 'green manure', but the meaning doesn't really sink in until you get involved in the art of composting. After making our first cubic metre of humus we understood the value of growing food for the compost heap. Composting artists can literally grow their own medium! – It's a bit like painters mixing their own pigments from natural materials.

Therefore the *Complete Compost Gardening Guide* wouldn't be complete if it didn't include a very useful chapter on 'Compost Fodder Crops'. The authors explain, "*Like the fodder crops that farmers grow to use as food for livestock, Compost Fodder Crops are plants that compost gardeners grow to feed the soil, either directly, as a green manure, or indirectly via composting projects. Hundreds of different plants can be used as fodder crops, but the best ones are superior for building soil and making compost.*"

However, not all soils are vegetarian or vegan. To supplement the plant-based diet, a healthy compost can benefit from waste products from the animal kingdom, especially manure from cows, horses, chicken and other farm animals. Many organic and biodynamic farmers consider cow manure indispensable for a good compost. Another valuable animal based supplement is worm castings – the excretions of earthworms. Some contemporary composting artists add a worm farm to their 'studio space' to make sure they have a ready supply of the precious substance produced by these little creatures.

Composting experts also recommend adding *ingredients from the mineral kingdom* as essential supplements to the compost. Lime, calcified seaweed, silica, rock dust, or clay are favourites to spice up the composting menu. Moreover, *charcoal*, or *carbon* – the porous black stuff you get when you burn wood in the absence of air – has played a starring role in the list of composting ingredients in indigenous (agri)cultures of the past and is now celebrating a revival.

The greatest of all crafts

"Farming is – or should be – the greatest of all crafts." Lord Walter James Northbourne, an English farmer and visionary wrote in 1938. *"A craft does not approach perfection until it merges into art. So it is with farming, in which perfection for its own sake must be the aim, though it be approached but gradually. Perfection means beauty; beauty in art is the flowering of the urge to perfection which exists somewhere in all of us."*

Considering the vast range of source materials, combined with our comparatively limited understanding of the creation of humus, the art and craft of composting as a creative pursuit is still waiting to be discovered. Composting virtuosos like

Maye Bruce, Sir Albert Howard and Marie Luise Kreuter would agree that this form of creative work is fulfilling, nourishing and life-enhancing at many levels. Like any good art or craft project, composting has the potential to raise awareness of our place in the cycle of life and the contribution we can make to regenerate the vitality of the Earth.

"*Every artist must first be a craftsman*" Lord Northbourne observed. "*Farming is the craft side of the art of living; that which we seem to have lost.*" About half a century later Marie Luise Kreuter warned, "*The situation on our planet is becoming more and more threatening. In our gardens, however, we can help to steer against this trend, everyone in their place, everyone on the piece of Earth entrusted to them.*"

Chapter 6

The Sacred Worm

It may be doubted whether there are many other animals which have played so important a part in the history of the world, as have these lowly organised creatures.

~ Charles Darwin ~

Reverence for the earthworm

When Cleopatra was the Queen of Egypt (47–30 BCE) the earthworm was declared a sacred animal. "*Egyptians were forbidden to remove it from the land, and farmers were not to trouble the worms for fear of stunting the renowned fertility of the Nilotic valley's soil.*" A few hundred years earlier, on the other side of the Mediterranean Sea, Aristotle had already recognised the skills of the earthworm as a 'master builder'.

In 1881 Charles Darwin – he was already famous by

then for his work on the *Origin of the Species* – surprised his readers with a book on: *The Formation of Vegetable Mould, Through the Action of Worms, With Observations on Their Habits.* ('Vegetable mould' was the common term for 'humus' in his day). Most scientists were not interested in the habits of earthworms and their production of 'vegetable mould', and Darwin's odd fascination with the lowly creatures was met with scepticism. Vermiculture – the breeding of earthworms – had not yet been invented, but his work became an inspiration for earthworm researchers and breeders in the 20th century and beyond.

In the 1940s the American physician and vermiculture pioneer Dr Thomas Jason Barrett turned a semi-desert hillside farm into a tropical paradise with the help of earthworms. He called the earthworm a 'high-speed humus factory'. In his book *Harnessing the Earthworm* he writes, *"Working through remote geological ages down to the present in practically unchanged form, the earthworm has been and is one of the great integrating, soil-building forces of nature."*

Earthworms as soil builders

The earthworm is a major 'composting catalyst'. There are about 3000 species of earthworms worldwide, and some of them specialise in the processing of decaying vegetable matter and animal manure. If a compost heap is built directly on bare soil, earthworms of the right type somehow find their way into the pile and do their transformational work.

In organic gardening and permaculture, earthworms have a central place as 'workers' of the soil. They are considered the most important producers of perma-humus. Their excretions, or 'worm castings', as they are called, look like miniature sculptures. These build an ideal soil structure for plant growth. Through networks of channels in the earth, dug by the worms, plant roots can spread easily and absorb the nutrients they need.

George Sheffield Oliver – another American doctor who switched careers and became a worm breeder – confirms that, "*Earthworms are nature's own means of soil building and conditioning. No orchard or garden can do its best without them.*"

Having studied the habits of earthworms for several years, the German zoologist Ulrich Klever comes to the conclusion that earthworms can greatly accelerate the natural production of humus. "*While nature requires five hundred to a thousand years to produce a layer of humus barely 3 cm thick,*" he writes, "*a sufficient number of earthworms can achieve the same within five years.*"

Breeding earthworms

Vermiculture is becoming increasingly popular for several reasons: it produces excellent organic fertiliser, creating humus in a worm farm is much easier and quicker than building a compost pile, and it requires very little space. A 'worm farm' consists of a stack of a few boxes, which can be kept in a corner of a balcony or basement. A reasonable population of such a miniature farm can handle impressive amounts of vegetable scraps, egg shells, egg boxes, shredded paper, even some leftovers from cooked meals, the latter of which would normally not go into the compost pile.

Earthworms are generally not fussy about what they are fed, as long as the materials are small enough and not too dry. However, earthworm breeder George Oliver observed that the animals get used to a certain type of diet and cannot be transferred easily to a different environment. *"Consistent experiments and research work brought to light the fact that earthworms are as much in need of the food on which they were raised as the fish is in need of water. It was found that compost-bred earthworms demanded decayed animal matter; those raised in soil containing decayed vegetable matter demanded humus."*

(Note: Presumably Oliver uses the word 'compost' in relation to decomposed animal substances and 'humus' in relation to decomposed vegetable substances.)

This means earthworms cannot be easily transferred from the closed and sheltered system of a worm farm to an open compost heap or 'released into the wild' of a new vegetable patch. They may disappear into the deeper layers of the subsoil or starve to death because they cannot adjust to a radically different diet.

If we want to introduce worms into a new environment, George Oliver recommends that we impregnate the soil with worm eggs. "*If the eggs of the compost worm are gathered and placed in a rich soil minus decayed animal matter, a large percentage of them will hatch and prosper.*" Various experiments have shown that earthworms need to hatch in the environment in which they are intended to work, then they can adapt themselves to the available food sources.

The gold standard of humus

The burrowing habits of the earthworm have many advantages for the cultivated land, especially in dry areas. George Oliver tells us that his orchard thrives on less than 50% of water compared with neighbouring groves. He observed that earthworms prefer the cooler soil under the trees and dig their burrows there. "*During irrigation; a large proportion of the water enters the soil through these burrows, with* the result that most of it goes under the trees where the roots can use it, while much less than usual is wasted out beyond the root zone."

Earthworms burrow channels into the earth reaching deeper than the biggest plough. They help aerate the soil thereby sustaining many creatures living underground. The worm channels also retain water and thereby help protect the soil life against drought and even bushfires; and in the case of flooding they allow surplus water to drain off.

Worm castings produce perma-humus of the highest quality. In his book *Der Regenwurm* (The Earthworm) Ulrich Klever praises the qualities of this 'miracle soil': "*The most important thing about this miracle soil is that the humus is perma-humus, a form which doesn't change over decades and centuries. A humus which doesn't become tired and which cannot be washed out by rain.*"

Apart from putting your kitchen waste to good use and getting high-quality organic fertiliser in return, there are many reasons for starting your own worm farm. Sepp Holzer draws attention to a point which is often overlooked: "*Along with the valuable humus and the numerous earthworms and worm eggs, breeding these useful creatures has yet another advantage: you will learn to observe and put yourself in the shoes of other creatures. Your ecological understanding and empathy will improve.*"

An entourage of loyal supporters

By now we know that earthworms are not doing all the 'sacred work' of converting decaying vegetable matter into super-humus all by themselves. They have a huge army of loyal supporters, most of which are invisible to the naked eye. When Raoul Francé wrote his book *The Edaphon*, he developed a whole system of orders, classes, species and families of the *edaphic organisms*. This included 327 different species, which had been identified by soil scientists and microbiologists until that time.

»*The permanent residence in the soil puts the organisms, which are dependent on it, into a highly peculiar situation...*« Francé wrote. Earthworms and all other subterranean creatures live in permanent semi-darkness, protected from direct sunlight and other climatic influences. They survive in a relatively sheltered environment, on a more or less diverse diet of plant and animal matter and in a fairly narrow temperature range. They need an even level of moisture and work ceaselessly to maintain their own ecosystem.

This is very important information for any aspiring composting artist, since **the most important practice in this earthy discipline is the art of cooperation**. To create good humus we are completely dependent on the work of the edaphon. The earthworms and their 'entourage' are the ones who do all the work for us, as it were. The best we can do, is provide optimal living conditions for them, look after them and make it easier for them to do their valuable work.

Chapter 7

Clay, Rock and Lava

The first thin blanket of parent material of humus which was spread over the surface of the earth in preparation for the birth of life was the deposit of star dust.

~ Thomas Jason Barrett ~

Popular literature about humus and composting offers a lot of information on 'organic matter' from the plant and animal kingdoms. This can give the impression that the mineral kingdom plays no significant part in making good humus. Nothing could be further from the truth. Minerals, found in clay, stones and volcanic rock, supply the soil with essential nutrients and important structural elements.

Tools for earthworms

The zoologist Ulrich Klever observed that earthworms often have small stones and grit in their stomachs. They swallow them along with a rotting leaf, or whatever else might be on the menu, and use them as tools to grind their food into a very fine paste. "*The prepared food pulp reaches the stomach and it is kneaded and crushed with the help of tiny stones gathered there.*"

George Sheffield Oliver remembers that clay played an important role in his grandfather's earthworm farm: "In the centre of the barnyard was the compost pit, which, in the light of my present knowledge, I now know to have been the most perfect and scientific fertilizer production unit I have ever known." All the manure and bedding from the farm animals were gathered regularly and dumped into the large compost pit. These contributed ingredients from both animals and plants.

The farm also had a pond, formed of fine-textured clay. "*Each spring the pond was drained and ... many tons of this clay were scraped out and dyked around the borders of the pond to weather for use on the compost heap.*" Whenever the layer of organic matter reached a depth of 12-14 inches (30-35 cm), several tons of the red clay were spread over the compost, while "*beneath the surface the earthworms multiplied in untold millions, gorging ceaselessly upon the manures and decomposing vegetable matter, as well as the mineral clay soil."*

The mixture in the compost pit at George Sheffield senior's farm contained everything the earthworms needed to complete their transformative work: animal manure, urine, rotting hay and straw and fine clay. A few months later the compost had been transformed into humus.

Nutrients for plants

In the early 20th century Rollin Anderson realised that 'something was wrong with the American soil'. He left his city life in San Francisco, moved back to his native Utah and acquired a piece of land described as *"a range of terraced hills with a pink sheen... rising two hundred to five hundred feet from the arid desert plain, all with a pinkish ore."* An analysis of a sample revealed that the 'pink rock' was *"a colloidal clay containing quantities of minerals very similar to the caliche of Chile and Peru from which the world's nitrates have long been mined."*

The scientist who analysed the sample had studied the mines in South America and developed the conviction that *"the benefit plants were deriving from South American nitrates was not from the nitrates themselves but from minute quantities of trace elements, which served as catalysts."*

The clay of the pink hills in Utah turned out to be Montmorillonite, which is particularly rich in minerals and trace elements. Rollin Anderson started to experiment with the powdery clay in his own garden and was very pleased with the results: "*Once you've tasted a vegetable grown with Azomite* you are spoiled for life. The beets in the control plot were juiceless and woody. The ones with Azomite dripped with juice and were tender at all ages of their growth. By fall, one measured seven inches across, just as tasty as the young ones. The same with tomatoes, cabbages and peppers...Here was a substance that gave results that you could see without the aid of any microscope*".

(*Rollin Anderson renamed the clay when he began mining it for commercial purposes. Azomite is Montmorillonite from Anderson's clay mine in Utah).

Medicine for the forest

In the 1970s foresters and ecologists began to worry about a mysterious disease of trees all over Europe. The death of the forests had been foreseen by Rudolf Steiner half a century earlier, but his warning had been dismissed as 'esoteric nonsense'. The devastation known as 'Waldsterben' (dying forest) was played down for many years until it could be no longer ignored.

In 1980 Rudolf Schindele, a manufacturer of fine

veneers in Austria, made a chance discovery when he had logging roads built through a small forested mountain he owned. The ground was metamorphic rock known as 'paragneiss' or 'primaeval rock'. During the road construction over 3 kilometres, some of this rock was reduced to powder by the heavy equipment and blown into the forest by the wind.

"Just four weeks later, the spruces in these areas, whose needles had been growing increasingly yellow, a sure sign of Waldsterben, were turning back to a radiant dark green. The total area of recovering trees extended over some 13 acres. During the next four years, new growth on the accidentally treated trees looked better and better." For Rudolf Schindele this was the beginning of a new thriving business in rock dust as a remedy for dying forests and as a soil enhancer on agricultural land.

About a century earlier the German agricultural chemist and physician Julius Hensel had made a similar discovery. While milling grain, he noticed one day that some stones were mixed with the flour. He sprinkled this stone meal into the soil of his garden and soon noticed a more vigorous growth of his vegetables. Also, apple trees, which had produced low-quality worm infected fruit, were now laden with juicy high-quality apples free from worms.

Julius Hensel published his discoveries, began to sell 'Stone Meal' and gained a number of enthusiastic followers, including the Grand Duke of Luxembourg.

One satisfied customer wrote: "*If the tree has sufficiency of this primitive substance under its roots it is not only fruitful, but no more sensitive to frost and diseases. Nor will it be infested as much by insects, as it will be healthy, having a pure sap.*"

Food for the soil

In the 1980s the Swiss farmer John Ruegg emigrated and bought a 10-acre farm in New Jersey. When he purchased the farm, neighbours assured him he would never be able to produce a decent crop of any kind. The soil was so worn out, it might have won an award for 'worst farm in the county'. Within three years of starting to cultivate the land, John Ruegg was raising flowers, shrubs and trees and harvesting fruit and vegetables that would be the envy of any farmer.

John Ruegg's secret to raising this dead little farm from the ashes was powdered lava. He had a whole collection of the pulverised volcanic rock. "*On the other side of the storehouse were bins containing different kinds of powdered lava, for lavas are not alike in their composition. Some contain more of one mineral than another. Some are totally lacking in certain minerals. Ruegg combined them to meet the requirements of the soil that he desired to fertilize. It was upon the proper combination of the minerals that the success of this method of fertilization depended.*"

As a young man, back home in Switzerland, he had already been possessed by the idea that volcanic soil produces a luscious vegetation, and the revived farm in New Jersey was the proof. He understood the lack of minerals in the soil as a kind of malnutrition, and lava proved to be just the kind of food his soil needed.

Sustenance for life

The American agronomist and ecologist John Hamaker believed that rock dust is the only chance of survival for our civilisation. In his book *The Survival of Civilisation* he wrote in 1982, "*crop soils are badly demineralised. The minerals that are left have been selectively leached by acidic 'fertilisers' so that the minerals in the food supply are not only in short supply, but some elements are virtually missing. This can only result in enzyme shortages. Enzyme shortages sooner or later result in the physical, mental and spiritual degeneration of nations.*"

John Hamaker was convinced that certain types of rock contain the perfect combination of minerals and trace elements to restore the health of our soils and thereby regenerate and sustain all life on our planet. He was also certain that no chemical laboratory can improve on the perfect mix of minerals and trace elements supplied by nature.

"*Obviously, there is no way to maintain good health by*

taking some of this and a pinch of that. We aren't smart enough. The only answer is to make sure that the soil contains an abundance of available elements from the total natural mixture, and let the microorganisms pick and choose what they want, so that the natural balance of nutrients comes up through the plant life to us. There is no legitimate excuse for continuing to degenerate in mind and body. We can have the best health the world has ever known."

This quote contains an important principle. Nature provides an abundance of everything, and millions of workers (be they worms, bees, or microorganisms) work hard and with great precision for an optimum result in any given environment.

John Hamaker's plea to use powdered rock for the survival of our civilisation has been ignored for decades. Now eco-gardening experts recommend rock dust preparations as additives for the compost heap. The fine powders increase the activity of microorganisms in the heap, so the organic matter can decay faster. Even small amounts of the grey dust act as a catalyst for the creation of high-quality colloidal humus with an increased capacity to store vital nutrients.

Detox for the garden

Preparations of clay powder, rock dust, and pulverised

lava are commercially available in different grades for a wide range of applications. Rock dust, mostly pulverised basalt or volcanic rocks, are promoted as 'soil supplements for ecological gardens to add mineral trace elements and improve soil structure'. Among other things, they help regulate the pH level in overly acidic soils.

Powders made from metamorphic or igneous rocks used in horticulture and ecological agriculture must be ground to their colloidal stage (i.e. into a very fine powder) to make the minerals and trace elements 'digestible' by the plant roots.

Montmorillonite clay is sold under trade names such as *Azomite* and *Bentonite* and promoted as a 'soil improver'. Among other things, clay increases the capacity of the soil to store water. Clay also binds heavy metals and other toxic residues in the soil from chemical and environmental pollution.

Bentonite and Azomite preparations can therefore be used as a 'detox for the soil'. Both clay varieties are also offered in higher grades of purity for internal use – as a dietary detox supplement – and in cosmetic detox-products such as skin masks and bath supplements.

In his book *Harnessing the Earthworm* Thomas J. Barrett wrote, *"The first thin blanket of parent material of humus which was spread over the surface of the earth in preparation for the birth of life was the deposit of star dust,... brought to the earth by the rays of the sun and other whirling bodies... throughout the infinite reaches of space."*

As our soils are increasingly faced with threats of pollution and erosion, powders of rock, lava and clay – like the original deposits of star dust – play a vital role in the regeneration of the earth.

Chapter 8

Schools of Composting

There are really as many recipes for making fruit compote as there are fruit compote makers – probably more. You'll find the same is true with composting.

~ Stuart Campbell ~

Many ways, one journey

In his book Let it Rot the American composting artist Stuart Campbell writes *"For too long there has been an air of cultist mysticism surrounding the art of composting. This is the kind of nonsense so many people find objectionable in a lot of composting literature. It is easy to get confused by gardening magazines and gardening books that describe the 'science' of composting in such narrowly defined terms that you get the distinct impression that there is one and only one, method for making humus."*

Humans all over the world have practiced composting long before Albrecht Thaer, Sir Albert Howard, Lady Eve Balfour, Maye Bruce and contemporary Western farmers and gardeners became fascinated with the transformation of organic matter into humus. The value of the earthworm was known in ancient Greece and Egypt. Farmers in India, China, Tibet and South America used their own organic composting methods for hundreds of years with great success and without any input from Western 'expertise'.

In the art of composting there are many ways to reach a similar result – rich and fertile humus. Below are brief descriptions of some common methods; the list is by no means complete. Suitable materials for any of these composting method are: twigs and small branches from hedge cuttings, grass clippings, raw vegetable waste from the kitchen, animal manure (if available), cardboard, paper, egg shells, coffee grounds, tea leaves, weeds, hay, animal bedding, autumn leaves, wilted flowers. For a mineral rich humus it is beneficial to add sprinklings of rock- or lava dust, clay, sand and/or garden soil to the mix.

A – Slow compost

"A compost is not a travelling circus," says Marie Luise Kreuter, implying that a compost pile or pen should live in one place. The location for the compost is in the shade, it sits directly on the soil, and it has a footprint of about 1 square meter.

Twigs and chopped up small branches are ideal for the bottom layer to ensure good drainage. Other materials are mixed and arranged in layers of about 20 cm (8 inches). Each layer is covered with a thin layer of soil. Depending on climate conditions the heap should be watered occasionally to keep it from drying out. This compost pile can build up over time until it reaches a desirable height (about 1 meter). The top of the compost heap is covered with a thicker layer of soil and left to mature, which can take between 6 months and one year.

B – Classic organic compost

This compost can be built in the same way as the 'slow compost', with two differences: (1) All materials are arranged in quick succession. This means the composting artist needs to have stacks or buckets of the materials ready to make a whole cubic metre of compostable layers. The layers are watered to ensure an even moisture content. The finished heap is covered with cardboard, an old carpet or any suitable organic material. With all the materials ready at hand it should take about 1-2 hours to complete the heap.

After 3 weeks the whole pile is turned over with a pitchfork, ensuring that the materials on the outside of the pile are placed into the centre. The turning of the pile is repeated twice in intervals of 3 weeks. After the third turning the organic compost is left to 'mature'. Depending on temperature and season, this can happen in as little as 3 months (i.e another 3 weeks after the third turning of the pile).

C – Container compost

Compostable materials can be collected in dedicated containers of various materials and sizes. When using a container it is important to ensure that the compost gets enough air, and the moisture content can be regulated, so it doesn't get too wet or too dry. To get started you could build a simple 'composting container' with 4 posts in the ground and a piece of chicken wire.

D – Biodynamic compost

This compost can be built in the same way as either the 'slow compost' (A) or the 'classic organic compost' (B) described above.

For a biodynamic compost you need the biodynamic preparations as a 'starter'. When building version (A) the preparations are added at the end by making 6 deep holes in the compost, 1 for each preparation. When building version (B) the preparations are added in the centre by making 6 small earth balls, each with one preparation inside, and placing them in the middle of the compost pile. The biodynamic compost is expected to be ready for use in the garden within 6 months.

(This is without taking into account the period needed for the preparations themselves.) Maria Thun's biodynamic garden calendar recommends that every compost mixture "*should rot if possible for a whole year so that the cosmic forces of an entire sun year can take its effect.*"

E – Permaculture compost

According to Bill Mollison, "*The only places where soils are conserved or increased are:*

- In uncut forests
- Under the quiet water of lakes and ponds;
- In prairies and meadows of permanent plants; and

- **Where we grow plants with mulched or non-tillage systems.**"

Permaculture gardeners don't advocate setting up dedicated composting plants, even though soil conservation and the production of nutrient-rich humus are a major focus. They prefer to emulate the natural process of soil formation which can be achieved through mulching, as an alternative way of composting.

"*Mulching also supplies the soil with valuable nutrients,*" Sepp Holzer writes. "*It is nothing other than surface composting; it involves spreading a layer of organic material over the soil to serve as ground cover. The soil receives a protective cover from this, which prevents it from drying out, becoming eroded or suffering from the extreme effects of weather.... In the mulch layer a constant process of decomposition takes place, through which the mulch is turned into high quality fertiliser."*

F – Surface compost

In his lectures on biodynamic agriculture, Alex Podolinsky explains a way of improving the humus layer in the soil which he calls '*surface composting*'. In agreement with Sepp Holzer he says, "*surface composting is much better, since the soils are grazed dynamically and stimulated dynamically.*" This method, however, is different from mulching. It has been developed for bigger farms with livestock; and it could potentially be adapted for smaller projects.

For a *surface compost*, organic matter is distributed directly over large areas. For example, cows are left to graze on a pasture for a limited time and drop their manure. After 10 days the herd moves on, the fresh cow dung is raked over the whole field, and the clover and grasses in the pasture are left to regrow. After reaching a certain ideal height, the plant cover can be cut and left as green manure for the soil. Additionally, biodynamic preparations are sprayed over the farmland at specific times.

With this method the soil structure and quantity of humus can be continuously improved within a relatively short time. Surface composting was used at Agrilatina, a biodynamic farm near Rome, and a 'miraculous soil transformation' happened within one year.

G – Bed compost

Bed composting was made popular by the permaculture movement under the name *sheet composting*. The compostable materials are arranged in layers over a larger and shallower area. A 'compost bed' can be built in situ to prepare a new vegetable patch or flower border, to suppress weeds and produce more humus, or to revive an existing garden bed. Bed compost is a hybrid between mulching and composting.

Composting artists and humus experts know that the earth should never be left bare. Nature makes sure that the topsoil is always covered with plants or 'organic waste'. Without this protective cover, part of the ecosystem is damaged or destroyed, and the cycle of regeneration is broken.

For a successful compost bed, Christa Weinrich recommends covering a designated area gradually with a mix of garden 'waste' as they become available.

Partially rotted materials from a slow compost (A) can be added to the mix. Fresh kitchen waste is *not* suitable for a bed compost, but shredded paper and cardboard can be used. Broken up green manure plants are ideal, and a layer of grass clippings makes a good cover blanket.

Barbara Pleasant and Deborah Martin suggest another method: Dig up grass sods from a lawn designated to become a new garden bed. The exposed soil is covered with small branches and twigs to a depth of about 10-20 cm (4-8 inches), the grass sods are placed upside down on the woody layer, and this is covered by a thick layer (20 cm/8 inches) of shredded plant materials.

Bed composting has three advantages. It rots relatively quickly, it produces nutri-humus where it is needed, and it saves the additional work of transporting the humus from the compost heap to the garden bed.

H – Humus storage ditches

On his permaculture farms, Sepp Holzer digs so-called 'humus storage ditches' at the bottom of a new terrace. Any surface water and soil that is washed down the slope gets caught in the ditches and is retained for the land. Valuable nutrients and humus are collected in the ditches during heavy rain, and these can be used for new plant growth. Moreover, the ditches have a positive effect on the water cycle of the the land because they provide additional water reservoirs.

I – Fast track compost

For a faster production of humus, all ingredients need to be cut as small as possible to help the earthworms and microorganisms do their work: fruit and vegetable peels must be chopped, egg shells crushed, leaves and twigs shredded, etc. The layers are built up as in the 'classic organic compost' (B). A plant based *composting catalyst* is sprinkled between the layers to activate the composting process. Depending on the temperature and season this compost can be expected to mature within 4-12 weeks.

K – Worm compost

All the methods described above can produce good humus. A very different method relies on the breeding of earthworms to make what Marie Luise Kreuter called 'super-humus'. Vermiculture has become popular in recent years. It is a composting system which can be used in relatively small spaces and independently of having a garden. A 'worm-farm' consists of a stack of boxes which can be kept in a basement, on a balcony, or even in a kitchen.

For a worm compost a supply of suitable earthworms,

or their worm eggs, are essential. The worms can be fed on a wide range of substances: kitchen waste, including raw vegetable materials and left overs of cooked meals, shredded paper, egg boxes, coffee grounds, tea leaves, left over tea and coffee etc.

Earthworms are relatively undemanding. As long as they are fed about once a week with suitable food stuff, they eat, reproduce and excrete their precious worm-castings – a perma-humus of highest quality.

L – Terra Preta compost

Terra preta literally means *black soil* in Portuguese. It was discovered in the Amazon region of Brazil; and in contrast to the *Black Earth* of the *chernozem* in Moldava and the Ukraine (see Chapter 1), *terra preta is manmade*. It was produced by the indigenous population of the Amazonian jungle by combining human manure with charcoal and allowing the mixture to decompose in closed clay vessels buried in the soil. The result was an extremely rich and deep humus layer, which maintained its fertility for hundreds of years.

Terra preta caught the attention of soil scientists and ecologists, since it produced incredibly fertile soils, despite – or in this case because of – intensive use of the land, while in other parts of the world, intensive agriculture usually seems to result in soil degradation. The most important ingredient, which gives terra preta its name, is charcoal. Small pieces of porous charred wood attract an abundant population of microorganisms which help decompose garden and kitchen waste, and the coal serves as an excellent water reservoir.

In recent years terra preta has been rediscovered as a 'new composting method' and is attracting a growing loyal following. What is now presented as *'terra preta compost'*, however, doesn't necessarily contain the same ingredients as its Amazonian namesake.

M – Bokashi compost

Bokashi is known as an *'indoor composting system that ferments and pickles food waste'*. The name *bokashi* is Japanese and means literally *'obscuring the direct effectiveness'*. As a composting method it refers to *'fermenting organic matter.'* Strictly speaking, bokashi is not a composting but a *fermenting process.* It can, however, produce valuable humus, therefore it is included here.

Bokashi works by adding so-called 'effective micro-organisms' to a bucket full of kitchen waste to stimulate the decomposition process. It is an anaerobic composting method and works in a closed system. Bokashi neither produces unpleasant smells, nor attracts unwanted animals. It can be used with small quantities of organic waste in a small apartment. These features make it particularly attractive for urban gardeners and anyone who doesn't have easy access to an outdoor composting installation.

The Golden Rule of composting

The German biodynamic gardener and humus expert Peter Berg offers four 'golden rules' of composting:

1 – **Shred everything**. All materials that go into the compost pile should be cut small (4 x 4 mm).

2 – **Mix it well**. Different types of materials should be mixed (soft with woody, dry with wet, half rotted with fresh etc.)

3 – **Keep it moist**. A compost heap should never dry out, but it mustn't get too wet either. Too much and too little water will interrupt the rotting process.

4 – **Keep it covered**. A compost mixture should be kept warm or at an even temperature which stimulates the rotting process.

These are important and very useful basic guidelines. However, the focus on composting methods and technical details inevitably draws the attention into the mindset of reductionist materialism. The composition of a compost pile is a unique opportunity to 'tune into the mind of the soil' as it were. The decomposition process is effectively the *gestation period of a living organism* which is eventually born in the form of *mature humus*. A 'good compost' is a healthy compost, and a healthy compost is teeming with life. Instead of focussing so much on materials and techniques, we can turn our attention to the microorganisms we want to attract to the pile.

A handful of good compost should be populated by billions of living creatures. So the primary purpose of the compost pile becomes to provide a great home for the right kind of little critters. This requires a more holistic way of thinking, and it leads to one Golden Rule: **make your compost a little paradise for the edaphon.**

Chapter 9

The Wholeness of Humus

We have tried to conquer nature by force and by intellect. It now remains for us to try the way of love.

~ Lord Walter James Northbourne ~

The result of any composting process is nutrient-rich humus, ready to impregnate your garden soil and plants with health. It is neither difficult to do, nor prohibitively expensive to make. Anyone can practice the art of composting. With the right mixture we can grow better, healthier food and at the same time do our bit to heal the exhausted soil mother.

Wendell Berry suggests: *"Make a little compost of your kitchen scraps and use it for fertilizer. Only by growing some food for yourself can you become acquainted with the beautiful energy cycle that revolves from soil to seed to flower to fruit to food to offal to decay, and around again. You will be fully responsible for any food that you grow for yourself, and you will know all about it. You will appreciate it fully, having known it all its life."*

You will also get to know humus all its life – from its birth, 'rising from the ashes' of the compost, to full maturity – and protect its immortality.

Many soil scientists seem to struggle with getting to know humus. It is indeed hard to grasp 'soil organic matter' by trying to analyse its components and figure out 'what it does' and 'how it works' by scientific means. This approach has lead to fundamental misconceptions and false definitions of humus as 'the very dead' and a 'non-renewable resource'. The materialistic paradigm cannot understand processes of life. The key to 'solving the mystery' of humus lies in viewing it as a living organism, rather than an 'organic substance'.

The colloidal state

When you look at humus as a living organism, or a *'natural body'* – as some soil scientists suggest – it soon becomes obvious that it is part of the greater organism we call soil. And the soil is part of the greater organism we call Earth. Several authors mention one particular quality in the context of the aliveness of humus:

In Chapter 4, Alex Podolinsky emphasised that *"humus is a colloid."* In Chapter 7 Rollin Anderson's Azomite mine in Utah was described as made of "*a colloidal clay....*" The American soil scientist W.L. Powers called the earthworm a '*colloid mill*'. Selman Waksman wrote: "*Humus ... forms a complex colloidal system.*"

This made us wonder, *what exactly is a colloid, and why is it relevant for our understanding of humus?*

The word *colloid* comes from the Greek words *kolla*, meaning glue, and *eidos*, meaning appearance or form. As the name suggests, a colloid is something that has the appearance of being glued together. Emil Ramann (1851 – 1926), one of the founding fathers of soil science in Germany, explains that *a colloid is not a substance but a physical state*. Colloids are far more common than the use of the word itself. It seems as if almost any substance can be in a 'colloidal state'.

Egg white, for example, is in a colloidal state when whisked into a stiff foam. The bubbles of egg foam 'appear to be glued together' by air. Gold can be in a colloidal state when it precipitates in water under an electric charge; as a result, microscopically fine particles of the metal (0.005 to 0.015 nanometers in diameter) are suspended in water. The gold particles 'appear to be glued together' by an electrical charge. Humus 'appears to be glued together', partly because all the different organic substances from the compost pile have been digested by earthworms and excreted in a homogenous form, and perhaps more importantly because countless life forms are literally 'holding it together'.

Emil Ramann also mentions that "All *plant and animal bodies consist in their majority of colloids.*" He goes on to explain how colloids 'grow older'. This is a characteristic of humus too, as all experts confirm. 'Young humus' has different qualities and capacities than a 'mature humus'. At a younger age, it is more vulnerable and impermanent, while older humus is more 'stable' and enduring.

In conclusion, it seems more appropriate to replace the question *what is a colloid?* and ask instead *when is a substance in its colloidal state?* The answer is, *when it is dynamic, when it is alive or at least it has some characteristic qualities of a living organism.* Colloids are relatively stable structures, but – like egg foam – they remain relatively vulnerable, and they can also die.

Humus as a hologram

Any description of a living organism in terms of its constituents lacks something essential, no matter how detailed, scientific and 'complete' the list of components appears, or how precisely its functions can be measured. There is a simple explanation for this quandary: A *living organism is infinitely more than the sum of its parts.* Even if an accurate account of a living organism in terms of chemical and physical elements etc. were possible, this interpretation misses the essence of the creature and cannot lead to any true and deep understanding.

In his 'Metamorphosis of Plants,' Johann Wolfgang von Goethe described how he saw all parts of a plant as expressions of the same essence. Rudolf Steiner saw plants as essentially the same as the earth – they grow out of the soil, are nurtured by it and feed back into it. Goethe and Steiner were holistic scientists. They understood and examined phenomena from the perspective of wholeness rather than by splitting them into the tiniest possible parts, hoping to reveal some hidden secret that 'made things tick'

Viewed through the lens of wholeness, *a handful of humus is a fractal of the earth*. In other words, it has characteristics similar to a holographic image – i.e. when broken into smaller parts each piece shows the complete image. In a comparable manner, *any amount of humus carries the essence of the earth as a living organism*. Humus is earth, not part of it, but in its totality. From the perspective of holistic science, the state of our soil, its humus content or lack of it, is an accurate holographic image of the state of our planet.

The way of love

As reasons for the vanishing of our soils one could readily list *human greed, exploitation of natural resources, abuse and rape of Mother Earth...*, but what are the reasons for such savage and hazardous behaviour? Why do we destroy the very foundations of our existence? The surprising and sad answer is probably: **lack of love**. Our connection with the soil has been severed; and the sufferings from the epidemic of lovelessness are so varied that it can go unnoticed for a long time. The disease is intimately connected with the soil apathy and ignorance syndrome since our health depends on the health and nutritious value of our food, and the health of our food depends on the health and vitality of our soils.

Lord Walter James Northbourne wrote, "*Nature is only terrible or squalid to those who don't understand her, and when misunderstanding has upset her balance. She is imbued above all with the power of love; by love she can after all be conquered, but in no other way.*"

Getting to know humus through love. To the uninitiated, this may sound like a strange proposal. Passionate gardeners and farmers have always done it. A friend once told me, when they sold their home and farm, the hardest thing to leave behind was her 'black gold'. She was referring to a large pile of humus she had created over many gardening seasons.

We now know for certain that 'understanding' humus by force has lead to severe deterioration of the quality and quantity of humus and a significant loss of topsoil. 'Understanding' humus intellectually, by being able to isolate, measure and name its mineral contents of calcium, phosphorus, sulphur, potassium, silica, magnesium, iron, sodium and so on – not to mention the components derived from plants, including carbon and nitrogen, acids and alkalines, amino acids and other proteins, cellulose and other carbohydrates, etc. – and to identify earthworms by numbers and species, aerobic and anaerobic bacteria and other microorganisms, soil fungi, insects, protozoa, algae and all the rest of the edaphon in unfathomed varieties... this is all very interesting and informative (or confusing as the case may be). But it doesn't necessarily enable anyone to produce nutrient-rich soil and grow healthy food. Moreover, it is hard to deny that this type of 'understanding' has added significantly to the degeneration and loss of our soils and is now threatening our survival.

Lord Northbourne's plea in *Look to the Land* ends with the words: "*We have tried to conquer nature by force and by intellect. It now remains for us to try the way of love.*" Almost 80 years have passed since these words were written, and the way of love is still largely uncharted. Relentless attempts to conquer nature by force and intellect are continuing to drive us to the brink of extinction. However, it looks like the times are changing. As mentioned earlier, 2015 was declared *International Year of Soils*, and that period was extended to the whole decade, from 2015 until 2024.

Paradise Islands

In the past there were no laws against raping the earth, no organisation to prevent cruelty against the soil mother, and when humus was pronounced dead, it didn't make headlines. This is no longer the case. Now we can read that *"The Global Agriculture Report pleads for an intensive renaissance of pedological knowledge... and demands a relinquishment of all forms of disregard of the fundamental value of fertile soils."*

Regeneration International has become a hub for a network of over a hundred organisations and initiatives worldwide dedicated to regenerative agriculture and/or the development of pedological knowledge (pedology is the study of the soil). More and more people are realising that we can't survive on low quality food produced in dead soils. Urban gardening is a growing movement, conventional farmers are switching to regenerative methods, and unconventional farmers are producing 'miraculous harvests'.

In 2004 Perrine and Charles Hervé-Gruyer started to grow food on a quarter acre plot in Normandie. Before returning to France and starting a new life, she had been working as a lawyer in Japan, and he had been travelling the world, teaching about ecology and indigenous cultures. In other words, neither of them had been farmers. In 2016, a mere twelve years after creating their permaculture farm *Le Ferme du Bec*

Hellouin, they published a book with the title *Miraculous Abundance: One Quarter Acre, Two French Farmers, and Enough Food to Feed the World.* Bec Hellouin has become a celebrated model of innovative, ecological agriculture in Europe, and is attracting international attention.

In 2018 humus – or the frightening lack of it – and the extinction of soils in many parts of the world *are* making headlines. The results achieved by the Hervé-Gruyers are astonishing, but they are not unique. Their results are 'miraculous' in relation to our living memory and present expectations. Meanwhile, several pioneering farmers and gardeners are reporting similar abundant yields through bio-intensive methods. They are working with soils in America, Norway, Austria, Argentina, Japan, India, Australia, Canada and elsewhere. They are demonstrating that small bio-intensive farms with minimal equipment can be 10 times more productive than their conventional counterparts using heavy machines; and they are living proof that this can be done *while regenerating the soil*, rather than destroying it. Edible landscapes, forest gardens, tiny forests and edible cities are sprouting everywhere. In other words, whenever humus is met *with love and intelligence*, humans can create islands of paradise.

Appendix

1 - Creating Humus

Humus is born when organic substances decompose, and compost can be made in thousands of different ways. Here is a simple way to 'make humus', keeping in mind that you actually can't make it. You are only the facilitator, or the 'composer of the compost'. Here is a simple recipe for making compost in a pot.

Ingredients and Hardware

Green plant mix – grass clippings and wild plants, also known as weeds. Chop everything small.

Earthy mix – 1 part topsoil and 1 part sand. Mix them together well.

Brown plant mix – 2 or 3 handfuls of twigs and/or wood shavings. Break twigs into small pieces.

Hardware – 1 large flower pot (10 litres or bigger), 1 tray under the pot, 1 old towel.

Setting up the Compost

1 – Put the brown plant mix in the bottom of the

flower pot.

2 – Add a layer of green plant mix,

3 – Add a layer of earthy mix,

4 – sprinkle with a little water to keep it moist

Repeat steps 2 – 4 until the pot is full, ending with a layer of moist earthy mix.

Cover the compost pot with the old towel, place it on the tray (to catch any liquid) and leave in a sheltered place (for example cellar or garage). If the compost pot is kept outside make sure it is protected from too much sun or rain. The compost shouldn't dry out; sprinkle with water if necessary.

The leaves, stems and branches of all plants are populated by bacteria and spores of fungi. This means some 'humus makers' are already in the compost pot. These soil creatures (microorganisms) turn the green plant mix into humus, and they immediately start to work.

The time it takes for this composition to turn into humus depends on the temperature and season. All microorganisms that do the decomposition work are most active in spring, early summer and autumn. A steady temperature of 15-30° C is ideal for them.

If you want your compost to turn into humus as fast as possible, keep the pot in a warm place (room temperature). To speed up the decomposition process even more you can add 'compost activators' to the mixture (see appendix 3: *Compost Activators*).

You can also add earthworms to this compost mixture (see appendix 2: *Food for the Edaphon*).

2 - Food for the Edaphon

Compost is a great food source for earthworms and many other soil creatures. Any compostable materials chopped up into very small pieces are suitable food for the compost population. As a professional worm breeder, Thomas Barrett supplied his earthworms with special food supplements. *"Corn meal has been found to favor the formation of egg capsules,"* he writes. *"Corn meal ensures a ration of carbohydrates, proteins and fats for the worms, so that they will be well nourished, regardless of the organic composition of the composted soil-building material."*

Here is his recipe for a worm compost, it can be added to any composting arrangements.

Thomas Barrett's Recipe for Earthworm-Food

10 litres animal manure (broken up fine)

10 litres vegetable matter (straw, hay, green manure, fruit and vegetable peels, finely chopped)

10 litres good topsoil (well sifted)

Half a pound of corn meal

Mix all ingredients well, add to the compost heap and sprinkle with rain water.

"*If worms are to multiply rapidly, they must have plenty of water. The compost should be kept moist through and through but not soggy wet.*"

Please note: Soil is added *to absorb odours and prevent overheating of the compost*. A large compost heap is often set up with the intention to *generate heat*, which accelerates the decomposition process and kills unwanted seeds. In a worm compost too much heat is not desirable; especially *if the worms are kept in a closed box*. It might kill the worms and other beneficial soil creatures.

3 - Compost Activators

The decomposition of the organic materials in the compost heap can be stimulated by adding special 'food supplements for the microorganisms'. If you have access to animal manure, then this is a good 'compost activator'. If you compost only plant-based materials, other supplements can be used to stimulate the growth of the population of beneficial microorganisms, especially bacteria and fungi.

Food for Fungi and Bacteria

Elaine Ingham offers the following useful tips in *The Compost Tea Brewing Manual*:

"*Additives that help bacteria most are simple sugars, syrups such as molasses.*"

"*Materials that help fungi more than bacteria are things like fruit pulp.*"

Some specific foods stimulate the reproduction and activity of beneficial microorganisms:

Protein meals, such as oatmeal provides food for fungi.

Rock dust provides mineral nutrients for all soil organisms.

Yeasts provide a complex mix of proteins, minerals and vitamins for bacteria and fungi.

Some plant materials seem to inhibit the activities of certain microbes and are better avoided as 'compost foods'. These are: garlic, onions, citrus oils, cinnamon, oregano and soy.

Recipe to Feed Microorganisms

1 litre warm water

500 g brown sugar

1 packet of yeast

Dissolve sugar and yeast in the water and pour over the layers of your compost.

4 - Maye Bruce's Homoeopathic Preparation

The Discovery of this Preparation

Maye Bruce experimented with the *plant preparations* recommended by Rudolf Steiner in his course on biodynamic agriculture and developed her own recipe. The result is a *homoeopathic preparation* which stimulates the decomposition process.

Bruce experimented with various dilutions, as described in Chapter 2 of her book *Common Sense Compost Making*:

"*I filled a number of glass jam jars with lawn mowings, chopped-up weeds, nettles and general vegetable matter. I treated them with the solutions in the following strengths: 1 in 10 : 1 in 30 : 1 in 60 : 1 in 100 – and then, urged by an impulse – 1 in 10,000…*

"*In fifteen days it was obvious that the 1 in 10,000 was by far the best, in fact, almost broken down to compost.*"

With this compost accelerator a compost heap can turn into humus within an average of 2 months. A smaller compost kept in a sheltered place at an even temperature (such as our 'simple Compost Recipe', see appendix 1) can be transformed into humus within 3-4 weeks.

Ingredients of the Preparation

1 ~ Chamomile (Matricaria Chamomilla) – May – September

2 ~ Dandelion (Leontodum Taraxacum) – March – September

3 ~ Valerian (Valeriana Officinalis) – June – August

4 ~ Yarrow (Acchillea Millefolium) – June – September

5 ~ Nettle (Urtica Dioica) – March - September

6 ~ Oak (Quercus Ruber)

7 ~ Honey

The Essences

From the plants 1–4 gather fresh blossoms before noon (the months indicate when the flowers can be found in the wild in England). Moisten the blossoms with rain water. Pound in a mortar. Wrap in muslin and press out the juice. Allow the sediment to settle, pass through filter paper until the liquid is clear and decant into a bottle.

From the stinging nettle the whole plant is used without the roots. Extract the juice in the same way as the blossoms.

Keep each of the extracts separate!

From a mature oak tree gather a small amount of outer rough bark. Grind the bark to a powder and pass through a sieve. Steep one dessertspoonful of the powder in 2 oz (56 ml) of rain water, stir well, leave for 24 hours, strain and bottle.

These 6 essences are stored separately in dark glass bottles in a dark, cool place.

Pure runny honey is used as the 7th essence to make the 'stock solution'.

The Stock Solution

Mix one drop of each plant essence with 1 ounce (28 ml) of rainwater.

Mix one drop of honey with 1 ounce (28 ml) of rainwater.

Shake both mixtures well and store in a cool place.

The Compost Solution

Take 1 teaspoon of each stock solution and mix them with 1 pint (approx. half a litre) rain water. This quantity is sufficient for 1 cubic meter of compost.

(For the 'Sample Compost Recipe' (see Appendix 1) 60 ml of this mixture would be enough.)

Shake well and leave for 24 hours before use. This liquid will keep for about 3 to 4 weeks.

Now the mixture is ready to be added to the compost.

Shake well again before use!

Application 1

If you are building a compost quickly all at once, sprinkle about one quarter of the activator over the first set of layers, the second sprinkling over the 2nd set, the third sprinkling over the third set, and the final one at the end.

Application 2

If you are building a compost heap over a longer period, you can also insert the activator into the finished composition. Make 4 to 6 deep holes into the compost with a crow-bar. Pour equal parts of the liquid into each hole, fill it up with dry soil and ram it down to prevent air pockets.

<u>Please note</u>: The recipe for this preparation was taken from Maye Bruce's first book *From Vegetable Waste to Fertile Soil.*

Glossary

Azomite: Tradename for a type of clay called *montmorrilonite* and found in a particular area of Utah.

Bentonite: A type of montmorrilonite clay.

Biodynamic agriculture: farming method introduced by Rudolf Steiner.

Biodynamic preparations: Preparations suggested by Rudolf Steiner for the stimulation of the rotting process of the compost heap. The following substances are prepared for biodynamic farming according to specific recipes: *chamomile, dandelion, stinging nettle, valerian, yarrow, oak bark, cow manure* and *silica*. Some additional ingredients include cow horns, stag bladders, and the intestinal tubes of a cow.

Camomile: *Matricaria Chamomilla.* Ingredient for a biodynamic preparation and the *Quick Return Compost Activator* (QRCA).

Colloid: a mixture of 2 or more substances that don't absorb one another but enter into a state of 'living relationship'. The active ingredients of a colloid are microscopically small and suspended in a carrier substance. This enables them to be dispersed over large areas and enter living tissues, such as plant roots and cells in the body. Humus is considered a colloid.

Comfrey: *Symphytum officinale*, comfrey contains many nutrients to stimulate plant growth. The leaves are valuable as a liquid fertiliser or as an ingredient for the compost heap.

Compost: general term for compostable organic matter; the random accumulation of organic materials; the skilful composition of compostable matter in a heap or container.

Compost activator: a catalyst for the decomposition of compostable materials into humus.

Compost heap: A pile in the garden where organic materials are gathered to decompose into humus. The compost heap is sometimes affectionately referred to as the '*heart of the garden*', or the '*belly of the garden*'.

Dandelion: *Taraxacum officinalis*. Ingredient for a biodynamic preparation and the QRCA.

Decomposition: the decay of organic materials in the

composting process

Earthworm: burrowing worm that lives in the soil, eats and digests vegetable matter and animal manure, and excretes worm castings, considered to be the most valuable type of humus.

Edaphon: the microorganisms in the soil; equivalent to the plankton in the sea.

Eisenia foetida: a species of earthworms suitable for vermiculture.

Fertility: the capacity of the soil to produce healthy, disease resistant plants and 'living food'.

Green manure: plants grown specifically for soil improvement, or as an ingredient for the compost heap.

Humification: the decomposing process of compost into humus.

Humofix: a variation of the *Quick Return Compost Activator*, developed and sold by the Abbey of Fulda, Germany.

Humus: the *'placenta of the earth'*, a vital organ of earth as a living organism. Humus is the result of decomposed organic matter. It ensures soil health and keeps it alive.

Indore method of compost making: Composting

method developed by Sir Albert Howard on his farm near Indore, India.

Manure: animal dung used as an ingredient for organic compost.

Nutritional humus: humus which releases its nutrients quickly.

Oak bark: Ingredient for a biodynamic preparation and the QRCA.

Permaculture: an agricultural method designed to create self sustaining ecosystem.

Permanent humus: humus which releases its nutrients slowly.

QRCA: see *Quick Return Compost Activator.*

Quick Return Compost Activator (QRCA): a catalyst for the decomposition of compost, developed by Maye Bruce and now sold in England by Chase Organics. QRCA contains the same plant ingredients as the biodynamic preparations: *camomile, dandelion, stinging nettle, valerian, yarrow, oak bark*, plus *honey.*

Stinging nettle: *Urtica dioica.* Ingredient for a biodynamic preparation and the QRCA. Chopped stinging nettle added to the compost heap is a compost activator.

Super-humus: a name for humus produced by earthworms.

Valerian: *Valeriana officinalis*. Ingredient for a biodynamic preparation and the QRCA.

Vermiculture: the breeding of earthworms in a worm farm.

Worm castings: the excretions of earthworms, a valuable *permanent humus*, rich in nutrients and microorganisms.

Worm hotel: a special box system for breeding earthworms.

Yarrow: *Achillea millefolia*. Ingredient for a biodynamic preparation and the QRCA.

Bibliography

"Nature is not concerned to give us simple lessons."

– Lady Louise Howard –

Balfour, Eve, *The Living Soil*, Faber & Faber, London, 1948

Barrett, Thomas Jason, *Harnessing the Earthworm, a practical enquiry into soil building, soil conditioning and plant nutrition through the action of earthworms*, Johnson Press, Boston, 2008 (orig. published 1947)

Berg, Peter, *Biogärtnern: Der Grundkurs*, Frankh-Kosmos Verlag, Düsseldorf, 2013

Berry, Wendell, *Our Only World*, Berkeley CA, 2015

Bruce, Maye, *From Vegetable Waste to Fertile Soil*, Faber & Faber, London, 1940

Bruce, Maye, *Common Sense Compost-Making, by the Quick Return Method*, Faber & Faber, London, 1946

Campbell, Stuart Duncan, *Let it Rot*, Storey Publishing, Vermont, USA, 3rd edn. 1998

Darwin, Charles, *The Formation of Vegetable Mould through the Action of Worms, with Observations of their Habits*, John Murray, London, 1881

Francé, Raoul Heinrich, *Das Leben im Boden & Das Edaphon*, Organischer Landbau Verlag, Kevelaer, 2012 (new edition in one book, orig. pub. 1913 & 1922)

Francé-Harrar, Annie, *Die Letzte Chance für eine Zukunft ohne Not*, Bayer-Landwirtschaftsverlag, Berlin 2008 (orig pub 1950)

Francé-Harrar, Annie, *Humus, Bodenleben und Fruchtbarkeit*, Bayer-Landwirtschaftsverlag, Berlin 1957

Heynitz, Krafft von, *Kompost im Garten*, Ulmer Eugen Verlag, Stuttgart, 2000

Holzer, Sepp, *Sepp Holzer's Permaculture: A Practical Guide to Small-Scale, Integrative Farming and Gardening*, Graz, 2004, Chelsea Green Publishing, 2011

Howard, Albert, *An Agricultural Testament*, Oxford University Press, London, 1941

Howard, Louise, *The Earth's Green Garden*, Faber & Faber, London, 1947

Ingham, Elaine, *The Compost Tea Brewing Manual*, The Soil Foodweb Inc., Oregon, USA, 2005, 5th edn

Klett, Manfred, *Principles of Biodynamic Spray and Compost Preparation*, Floris Books, Edinburgh, 2006

Klever, Ulrich, *Bergmann des Ackers, die wunderbare Geschichte vom Regenwurm*, Verlag Sebastian Lux, Munich, 1951

Koons Garcia, Deborah, *Symphony of the Soil*, Film, 2012

Kreuter, Marie Luise, *Der Biogarten*, BLV, München, 1995 (17th ed.)

Krupenikov, Igori Arcadie et al, *The Black Earth, ecological principles for sustainable agriculture on Chernozem soils*, Springer Dordrecht, Heidelberg – London – New York, 2011

Mollison, Bill, *Permaculture: a Designer's Manual*, Tagari Publications, Tasmania, 1988

Nelson, Joshua, *Worm-Composting*, Storey Publishing, Mass. USA, 1998

Northbourne, Lord Walter James, *Look to the Land*, Dent, London, 1940, (repub. Angelico Press, 2003)

Oliver, George Sheffield, *Friend Earthworm*, Langford Press, CA USA 1941 (Online Library Journey to Forever)

Pfeiffer, Ehrenfried, *Anleitung für die Kompostfabrikation aus städtischen und industriellen Abfällen*, Gustav Fischer Verlag, Stuttgart, 1957

Pleasant, Barbara & Martin, Deborah, *The Complete Compost Gardening Guide*, Storey Publishing, Mass. USA, 2008

Scheub, Ute & Schwarzer, Stefan, *Die Humusrevolution*, Oekom Verlag, Munich, 2017

Shapiro, Howard-Yana & John Harrison, *Gardening for*

the Future of the Earth, Bantam Books, New York, 2000

Solomon, Steve, Gardening when it Counts: Growing Food in Hard Times, New Society Publishers, BC Canada, 2005

Steiner, Rudolf, Agriculture Course: The Birth of the Biodynamic Method (orig. pub. Koberwitz 1924), new edn. Dornach, Switzerland, 2016

Stewart Amy, The Earth Moved: On the Remarkable Achievements of Earthworms, Algonquin Books, North Carolina, 2004

Sulzberger, Robert, Kompost, Erde & Düngung, BLV, Munich, 2016

Thompson, Kenneth, Compost: the natural way to make food for your garden, DK Penguin Random-House, New York, 2007

Thun, Maria, Aussaattage 2018, Wetzlar, Jahrgang 56

Tompkins, Peter, and Bird, Christopher, Secrets of the Soil, new solutions for restoring our planet, Harper & Row, Alaska, 1998

Waksman, Selman, Humus: Origin, Chemical Composition, and Importance in Nature, Williams & Wilkins, Baltimore, 1936

Waldin, Monty, Biodynamic Gardening, DK Penguin Random-House, London, 2015

Waldock, Harold, *An Introduction to Permaculture Sheet Mulching: Experimental Strategies and Techniques for the Pacific Northwest Coast*, Edible Landscape Creations, Vancouver, 3rd end 2001

Weinrich, Christa, *Kompost, Gold im Biogarten*, Abtei Fulda, Germany, 2017

Weinrich, Christa, *Geheimnisse aus dem Klostergarten*, Stuttgart, 2017

Wrench, Guy Theodore, *The Wheel of Health: The Study of a Very Healthy People*, C.W. Daniel, London 1938

Wrench, Guy Theodore, *Reconstruction by Way of the Soil*, A Distant Mirror, 2017 (orig. pub. 1946)

Links

https://thehumusproject.org/

https://www.pssurvival.com/PS/Composting/Common_Sense_Compost_Making_1946.pdf

http://www.qrcompostingsolutions.co.uk/the-qr-system.php

https://www.chaseorganics.co.uk/products-for-gardeners/qr-compost-activator/

http://www.abtei-fulda.de/gartenbau/humofix.html

http://www.globalagriculture.org/report-topics/soil-fertility-and-erosion.html

https://www.fermedubec.com/

http://www.humusrevolution.de/

http://www.regenerationinternational.org/

http://journeytoforever.org/farm_library.html

http://thewormisturning.com/

About the Author

We do not inherit the Earth from our ancestors, we borrow it from our children.

~ proverb ~

Veronika Bond was born in a small village in Germany in 1955. Three years later, her family emigrated to Bethlehem (Jordan at the time), and she grew up in a boarding school for Palestinian orphans.

Back in Germany she studied Arabic in Berlin, German literature in Münster, and received a degree in Applied Linguistics from the university of Mainz. She went on to work as a freelance translator of modern Arabic literature for several years. After completing a second degree in classical homoeopathy in England she discovered that her translation skills were in great demand in this field, and she launched a successful career as a translator for homoeopathic literature.

In 2007 Veronika and her husband Joshua Bond visited Central Portugal for the first time. Soon afterwards they bought a 'Quinta', following a dream to live 'closer to the land', and grow their own food. Gardening in Portugal was more difficult than expected, partly because of their lack of experience as vegetable growers and partly because of the poor quality of the soil on their farm.

Cultivating an 'edible landscape' on degraded soil is a challenge as well as a unique opportunity to get to know the soil kingdom first-hand. Through her research, Veronika discovered how little known this important topic is today.

We owe our current knowledge of *humus as a living organism* to the pioneering work of men and women who dedicated their lives to understanding the soil. Many of them lived in the nineteenth and twentieth centuries. Some of their writings were hard to find and their names nearly forgotten.

Several eminent authors in this subject area, such as the microbiologist Raoul Francé, wrote in German, and their books have never been translated into English. Much of their contributions would have been lost, if it hadn't been for the increasing interest in permaculture and the urgent need to recover dying soils worldwide. Veronika's linguistic skills, combined with a personal interest in the developing field of eco-culture, provide the fertile soil from which this book has grown.

About this Book

It's the little things citizens do that will make a difference.

~ Wangari Maathai ~

Humus is the most precious resource on earth. Our survival depends on it, and it is running out. Dramatic losses of fertile soils are caused mostly by human activities. But *humans can also help regenerate humus.*

We have lost our relationship with the earth and forgotten how to take care of our soils. Humus has become a commodity, sold in garden centres and supermarkets. However, the familiar brown substrate in plastic bags is a far cry from the living organism described in this book.

HUMUS, *the black gold of the earth* is an invitation to become Earthkeepers. If we want to take care of Mother Earth – and perhaps grow our own healthy food – then we must get to know her better. We must learn to feed the soil first.

What makes the earth come alive?

What kinds of food does the soil need?

In what environment can the soil-population thrive?

These are some of the questions explored in this book.

Everybody can do something to take care of our soils and keep the earth alive. It is easier than you might think.

"This book is a riveting journey into where it all begins, the centre of life, the humus in the soil, this great mystery that feeds and protects us all. The book goes deep and sheds light on how life is created right under our feet. It gives clear examples, showing how to nurture humus and sustain the soil.

The importance of this book cannot be overstated – after all without humus there would be no life!"

Asa Mark & Hilary Bain,

the makers of the film

The Worm Is Turning

Zeitfracht Medien GmbH
Ferdinand-Jühlke-Straße 7
99095 Erfurt, Deutschland
produktsicherheit@kolibri360.de